BEING AN ADVOCATE DURING HOSPITALIZATION

*A Practical Guide To Being An Advocate
For Yourself Or Someone Else
During A Medical Crisis Or
Hospitalization*

Nancy McClellan
Tasi McClellan, BS, RRT

PublishAmerica
Baltimore

First printing

ISBN: 1-4137-0254-6
PUBLISHED BY PUBLISHAMERICA, LLLP
www.publishamerica.com
Baltimore

Printed in the United States of America

SPECIAL THANKS

A special thanks to Michael McClellan for his countless hours spent in support of our book.

TO THE READER

The information in this book is to assist those individuals who are in a hospital or care facility as a patient, advocate, or both.

To be aware, prepared and diligent as a patient or advocate, gives you control, input, and safeguards when a stressful medical situation confronts you.

TABLE OF CONTENTS

PREFACE

Early on a cool November morning, after driving all night, my daughter and I walked into my mother's hospital room as she waited for her imminent second bypass surgery. She had been taken the morning before to the hospital in congestive heart failure. Two months earlier she had been taken to the hospital with breathing problems, due to complications of congestive heart failure. After many long hours and many more tests she was sent home and told to increase her laxis. This medication rids the body of retained water.

The contrast between my mother's hospital experience during her hip surgery four years prior and the events that were about to transpire became more evident during the committed journey we both would finish.

That morning my mother's heart doctor came in and out of her room much too quickly. I was still adjusting to the realities of the situation and suffering from sleep deprivation. I didn't ask the questions that should have been asked and answered. My mother was much too agitated and nervous to ask the right questions for herself.

This was much different from the previous bypass surgery, or even her hip surgery, as she waited to be taken to the operating room. I asked about the anesthesiologist and learned that no one had talked with her the night before, nor had anyone seen her that morning. I checked with the nurse to see if something had been prescribed to relax her and keep her calm. The answer was an ominous, "No." I immediately requested that the nurse page a doctor and get something for my mother. Unbelievably, this dear woman, who did not ever want to go through this surgery again, had been given nothing to calm and relax her. Twenty or so minutes later, after trying to reach three different doctors involved in my mother's case, the nurse had not received one returned call or page. The call came for the transport of my mother to surgery. My mother's agitation now increased and the reality that she was going to surgery was evident in the fear that reflected clearly in her tearful eyes. After proceeding about twenty feet down the hall, the nurse was paged and told to wait. This was almost too much for my mother. She was pleading with me to make this go away, and maybe in hindsight, she knew more than anyone at this time what the end result was to be. I just tried to calm her and talk positive about what she was soon to endure and how much more energy she would enjoy.

I later learned that I could have canceled the surgery, until the situation was handled in a more humane way, so that the anesthesiologist could give medication the night before, and if needed, the morning of surgery. I am sure that a doctor would have arrived quickly if indeed I had said, "I'm canceling this surgery, take my mom back to the room, this has not been handled with her needs and comfort as the first concern." This is a right that you have when the medical situation is lacking compassion and the patient is suffering unnecessarily.

The second day after surgery, my mother was sitting up and very alert. This was one of just a few conversations that I had with her throughout the whole ordeal where she seemed like her old self. Then, over the next few days, she began exhibiting symptoms of decline. I began giving the vitals (blood pressure, heart rate, temperature, etc.) to my daughter-in-law, a respiratory therapist. As my mother's numbers became more alarming, my daughter in-law alerted me that she was in kidney failure. I immediately consulted with the ICU nurse who said she too had concerns about my mother's condition. I asked what could be done. The nurse suggested getting a kidney specialist involved. I instructed the nurse to do just that. A kidney specialist came within the hour. Why did I have to intervene to get this needed specialist into this health crisis? Where was the heart doctor, her primary care physician, the surgeon, or the lung doctor?

It took many days to pull her through the critical kidney complications. My mother then developed intense abdominal pain, so an x-ray was taken. Apparently there was more on the x-ray than the doctor initially told me, although it did confirm pancreatitis. After asking the nurse what the x-ray showed, I learned about a growth that had been revealed. I confronted her heart doctor about this new finding and he told me, "We can't be concerned about that right now."

Two and one half weeks after the bypass surgery, the cardiologist who had stabilized my mother's heart medication after her 1998 hip surgery, was covering for her current heart doctor. He had essentially saved her life at that time through medication that regulated her blood pressure. Upon reading her chart, the doctor was appalled that we didn't know if this growth was cancer or not, especially since one of her main complaints of pain was in her lower abdomen. The cardiologist requested the nurse to call an oncologist. Two weeks since the first x-ray in ICU and still not knowing the initial results, my mother had an ultrasound and more x-rays. The oncologist felt it was not a cancerous growth, although a biopsy was not taken. The pain in my mother's lower abdomen continued and increased until only morphine could give her relief. My mother's primary care doctor said that the tumor would require surgery as soon as possible. Two weeks is a long, long time when one is waiting to know about a loved one's possible cancerous growth, yet without a biopsy what did I really know for sure?

My mother was now locked into the never-ending cycles of her blood pressure being to low, complications with her heart and kidneys, and her lungs filling with fluid. To compensate for her low blood pressure, the doctors had to give her more fluids; which in turn caused a problem because her heart and kidneys weren't functioning properly; thereby causing her lungs and extremities to fill with fluids. This was outwardly evident as I observed her swollen ankles, knees, wrists and hands. The doctors would then give her laxis to rid the body of this excess fluid, which would in turn drop her blood pressure too low. Chest x-ray, after x-ray, never ending breathing treatments — her stressed body was in a cycle with no positive end in sight.

There was no physical therapy, and sitting in a chair happened only four times in two weeks. My mother couldn't eat because of her medical condition, and thus she had no strength, which prevented aggressive physical therapy. My mother's lower left abdominal pain continued to give her great discomfort and even increased as the days went by.

The nurses in intensive care were wonderful. They had fewer patients to care for at one time. Outside of intensive care a few nurses and their aids were wonderful, but it was so different from my mother's hospital stay four years prior. During this hospital stay, the nursing assistant did the vitals, and saw my mother throughout the day, while the registered nurse came only to give medications or deal with a serious problem. I got to know the nurses. These dedicated individuals gave me insights and information that allowed me to talk with the doctors and get results.

The first time the nursing assistant got my mother up they dropped her on her knees. This was a setback, and anytime after that she became fearful whenever they wanted to get her up. It would take two people to put her in a chair. She was weak and retaining a lot of water, which made movement even more difficult due to her swollen extremities.

I continued to give my daughter-in-law the vitals and this helped prepare me for the continual decline in my mother's condition. Her doctors were positive and just said, "Well, you must remember her age and it is just going to take longer for her health and strength to return." The bypass surgery was a success, but my mother still had a problem in her heart. I confronted her heart doctor about her decline and an echocardiogram was done. I asked the cardiologist if they found anything and he indicated that everything looked good. I found it hard to believe this was the case, considering my mother's declining condition.

Since my mother didn't need the equipment that monitored her heart, she was moved to what I called the holding floor. They hold you until you are transported home, to a long-term care facility, or you die. The care was minimal and I had to be there from early morning to evening. That way she wasn't left waiting in pain, in need of a bedpan, and I could ensure her other needs were met.

My mother had two great friends, a man and his wife, that would come in the evenings and stay with her for several hours. These wonderful angels gave me a much needed break. At one point they left town for over a week and I sure appreciated their help even more during the many weeks previous. My mother died the day they returned home. This was very sad for them, since they loved her as a dear friend. A younger woman friend came when she could and that allowed me to tend to the yard and other house chores. My mother did not have the energy for people and she was a people person, a "party girl," and president of a community women's club for many years at the time of her passing. This lack of not wanting her dear friends to come visit, told me all I needed to know about what was happening to her. I believe she knew her days were numbered and didn't want her friends to remember her that way.

Many times my mother seemed to be in her own little world. Her mind had always been sharp and clear, and now she often became confused. When I told her she had been in the hospital for four weeks, she refused to believe me.

About a week before she died, the cardiologist who had helped us know about the growth in her abdomen was again covering for her heart doctor. I saw him coming from my mother's room and went down the hall to meet him. I said, "The surgery did not correct what was wrong with my mom."

He was cautious, yet being an honorable man, answered me in this way, "I was not consulted about your mother's surgery. I knew about it after the fact. I would have liked a consultation with all the doctors and with the family."

I commented, "She never should have gone through this surgery, she still has the same problem and it's in her heart not her arteries."

He smiled and we walked towards my mother's room. I knew then that she needed to be released to go home, something that she kept asking me to do. I used the incentive of being able to go home to get her to eat and to try and sit in a chair. I would tell her, "If you eat mom and get your strength up, I can take you home. I can't lift you mom, you have to get strong." She tried to eat, but she just couldn't. She figured out she could go home in an ambulance and so we had the discussion of her going home. I asked for a consultation with someone who gives you information on the various care options outside of the hospital. She contacted hospice for me and a meeting was arranged the next morning. My mother knew nothing about the hospice arrangements. Because she didn't eat very well after her first bypass, she was not alarmed about her poor eating during this last hospital stay. In her mind the doctor would release her sooner, because she would start eating in her own home environment where she was comfortable.

Once hospice was a definite go for the next morning, I asked that all medications be stopped, except for pain. Her primary care physician she had for years agreed, and the focus from that point on was for a pain-free existence. The one statement that I made several times to her heart doctor was that I wanted her pain free. "Oh absolutely," he said. Unfortunately for my mother, he did a poor job in keeping that promise.

That night a call came. The nurse thought my mother was dying, and I was to go to the hospital. My son and daughter came to go with me and we arrived to find her having a breathing treatment and somewhat alert. She finished the treatment and we were able to visit with her. She seemed stronger than earlier that day and I sent my children back to my mother's house to sleep while I stayed behind.

She remained awake most of that night, with a vivid imagination. She had me folding clothes, sweeping the floor, and getting the cobwebs off the walls among a list of other chores that she needed done. Sometimes she would sleep for 20 minutes or so and then she would talk and talk and have me do various tasks.

Morning came and my son and daughter returned to the hospital. They called another sibling, my daughter Christine, who lived further away, but had been with me the most through this journey and provided me with a great deal of welcomed support. When she arrived the other two prepared to return to their families. Their tearful goodbyes told me that they knew they would most likely not see their grandmother alive again. Her doctor asked me to postpone taking her home that day since she had such a bad night. I agreed and called the hospice counselor to arrange things for the following morning. The doctor also agreed that there would be no more breathing treatments.

Once I had decided on hospice, I never saw any of her other doctors, only the physician she had been going to for more than twenty years, who was actually semi-retired at the time.

The doctor had ordered morphine from that point on. My mother had constant bouts with pain in her lower abdomen that required pain meds as often as possible. The doctor had left and she began an agonizing ordeal with the pain in her abdomen that was worse than anything she had experienced prior. I went to find the nurse, who said the morphine was "stuck" in the medication drawer, which was where all medications were held upon receipt from the pharmacy. She gave her a pill by mouth to compensate. Time passed and the pain was still extreme. I went to find the nurse again. It took a while to talk with her, because she was busy giving out medications. I explained my mother was really hurting, and the nurse said she'd bring another pain pill. That did nothing, and the morphine was still "stuck" in the medication drawer. My mother was pleading for relief while my daughter was rubbing her back as she was nearly in a fetal position. My daughter had tears coming down her cheeks and my mother was hurting beyond anything that I had ever witnessed. I took out my cell phone and called her doctor. I explained the situation to the doctor's answering service and said, "I need him to call the nurse right now, and tell her what to give my mom." I told my daughter, "I'm going to find the nurse, because when the doctor calls I want to make sure she gets the call."

The nurse was on the phone to the doctor when I walked up to the desk and I heard her tell him that they just got the drawer "unstuck" and they have the morphine, but she had already given my mother two pain pills. The doctor must have been telling her to give my mother the morphine, but the nurse kept insisting that she had already given her two pain pills. The nurse listened intently for about thirty seconds, and then said, "Yes, doctor, right away." She got her shot and within ten minutes was comfortable. We visited as she was slowly drifting off to sleep. I gave her one last kiss and said, "I love you, Mom." Her smile was tender and she was peaceful.

She never woke up after that. When the pain would start, the shot would send her to that peaceful, pain-free place.

I had not slept for thirty-six hours. I told my daughter about eight o'clock that I had to go to bed. I slept at my mother's house where the phone was by the bed. The call came in the middle of the night. The nurse who was on duty that night was the same one that had called the night before, so she was very vigilant. I didn't leave for the hospital right then as I knew she was happy and with loved ones who had gone before. I knew I had major decisions that required an alert mind, and I was able to peacefully return to sleep.

We arrived at the hospital about six in the morning. Arrangements would be made later as to what mortuary would take care of her. The nurse said that she had checked her often and that she passed on very peacefully. We were very thankful that she did not struggle as sometimes happens, nor was she aware that she was taking her last breaths.

I watched many dedicated nurses trying their best to give compassionate and competent care. But there are too many patients with so many needs. These people are truly angels, yet we will lose them from our medical facilities as too much is being demanded from them.

There were many doctors too, but this time with my mother, her health situation was like a puzzle and there was no one looking at the whole picture, only the pieces they had added. I feel this compromised her treatment and care, which caused unnecessary suffering.

Because my mother had come into the emergency room in congestive heart failure and had successful bypass surgery previously, the primary care doctor and one heart doctor made the decision for the immediate second bypass surgery. There should have been a meeting with all her doctors and the family. Information is vital when making life and death health care decisions. Get as much information as you can so that you can ask the right questions and make informed decisions.

I share this with you because you have the right to know all the medical facts, as well as request a consultation with all the doctors that treat the patient. Often we are just told what is to be done, without discussion about alternatives, advantages and disadvantages.

What about the patient's preferences? If they are not competent, then the legal advocate needs to declare this because they should have already discussed the many variables and options of a medical crisis with the patient. It may also already be legally outlined and the medical personnel should be made aware of this.

Does the patient fully understand the doctor's decision? I recognized that my mother was not physically healthy enough when this decision was made to voice any questions or concerns. I arrived the morning of surgery. I knew her heart doctor and primary care physician because of past medical situations. I trusted their judgement and did not ask for a consultation with her other doctors to weigh the grave decision involving heart surgery for an older woman with other medical problems.

Complex medical crisis have greater health consequences, thus, information, knowledge, consultations, discussion and clarity provide a patient/advocate control and input that certainly gives one considerable peace in an often intense situation. Informed decision making promotes quality health care and it perpetuates a higher medical standard.

I had been through five hospital experiences with my mother. I had learned much over the years. This last hospital experience was so disheartening and frightening. Everyone needs an advocate in a medical situation. My mother's hospital happened to cater to celebrities and the wealthy. It is considered one of the best. Unfortunately, the best no longer exists in our hospitals and that is a sad commentary on the value we now place on suffering and life. Learn from my experience and ignorance. I have.

CHAPTER 1
I AM AN ADVOCATE

I AM AN ADVOCATE

What does an advocate do? Through my experiences with my mother in hospital situations over the past twelve years and my co-author's knowledge and experience within the medical field, we hope to give you invaluable information as to what an advocate does. We know that the information within this book will enable you to be a confident patient, advocate or both. While this book is written from the standpoint of you as an advocate for someone else, the information is just as relevant when you find yourself in a medical situation that requires you to be an advocate for yourself. It also helps you understand the importance of an advocate understanding your wishes and desires now rather than waiting until you are in the middle of a medical crisis, when it may be too late.

My mother underwent bypass surgery, pacemaker surgery, hip replacement surgery, hernia surgery and a second bypass surgery all within a twelve year period. She was seventy-one years old when she had her first bypass surgery and eighty-two when she had her second.

For the first bypass surgery, my stepfather was alive and we both shared the responsibility of the hospital stay and home recovery. My stepfather died before the other surgeries, so it was just my mother and I. Needless to say it was a journey for both of us with highs and lows, but a bonding experience that can't be adequately described. Anyone who becomes the parent to the parent, or needs care as now the child, can relate. Few could describe the feelings and the strangeness of it all.

My mother's hip had been fused since age seven due to a bike accident. Thus her hip surgery was innovative, complicated and needed, because her hip could no longer support the weight of her upper body and she would soon be in a wheelchair. She was a socially active woman, who belonged to many clubs and was always on the go. Being immobilized in a wheelchair would have caused her to emotionally decline into a state of nothingness.

I have witnessed the slow and subtle decline in the quality of hospital care over the past twelve years. The decline is alarming and frightening. In the September 2001 *Reader's Digest*, an article entitled "Hospitals Gambling With Your Life" addresses this serious situation.

One major reason for the decline of quality medical care is simply money. The rising costs of medical facilities and supplies, combined with lower reimbursements from insurance, have had an increasingly significant impact. The changes are obvious and evident to hospital care workers, and anyone that has had numerous hospital stays over the past five to ten years.

Through our experiences, we will share with you how being prepared and becoming familiar with the functions of the hospital, knowing your rights, and understanding your options after the hospital stay, will help you become an advocate with confidence.

THE NEED FOR AN ADVOCATE

When my mother had hip surgery in 1998 she had a Registered

Nurse (RN), a Licensed Practical Nurse (LVN or LPN), and a Certified Nursing Assistant (CNA). She also had this competent care and assistance with her first bypass surgery. In both the first bypass surgery and hip surgery hospital stays, the room had a board, which contained the names and the titles of those who would be caring for her every day and evening. During my mother's last hospital stays, there were no boards to help me know who her daily nurses were, and no LPN's. Staffing has changed dramatically. Health care workers are being stretched to their limits. One of many reasons behind the medical staff being stretched is that hospital budgets are being cut. Reimbursements from insurance companies and government Medicare and Medicaid are being cut, not allowing for the money necessary to pay for enough qualified nurses to assist and meet all the needs of the patients. This has caused the ratio of patients to nurses to increase greatly. This makes it harder to receive the individualized, quality care that is needed. The March/April 2002 issue of *Good Housekeeping* magazine contains an article entitled "Where Are The Nurses?" which provides insights into this problem.

There is also an increase in time being spent in documentation for reimbursements and protection against lawsuits, which has taken the medical care workers time away from time they should, and could, be spending taking care of patient needs.

A typical scenario outside of an Intensive Care Unit (ICU) would have one RN for every 3-8 patients, depending on the acuity of the patients. This one registered nurse would have to meet all the medical needs of the patients as well as administer drugs, contact doctors, and make sure procedures have been done. To help the RN is an assistant, called a CNA. Some hospitals still have licensed practical nurses (LPN or LVN), but they are limited in the care they can provide. To cut costs, hospitals are now hiring certified nursing assistants to assist the registered nurses. The CNAs will be assigned to change bedding, help with restroom needs, sanitary needs, all personal care needs, eating and taking vitals. A CNA or LPN will be assigned up to 3-8 patients. The CNA has very little schooling; it only takes a six-week course to complete your CNA certification. If they are busy and/or don't have the experience to know that the medical needs of a patient aren't being met, the patient's condition can deteriorate quickly. The CNAs have had to become the eyes and ears of the RN.

Stretching medical staffs so thin causes communication barriers between staff and patient. The need for an advocate is great. Someone is needed that can coordinate all the superfluous information and care, leaving the patient only to worry about those things that are really important to their health and well being.

DECISIONAL CAPACITY

It is important that an individual make choices for themselves. That ability doesn't necessarily go away because of an illness or because of age. However, some people may not be able to make sound decisions because of other factors. Some of those factors include:

Medication
Fear
Pain
Depression

People in these situations may need to have others help them with their decisions. This can be a ominous and difficult burden for someone to bear. Because of that, it is important for those who may have to make those decisions to know the wishes of the patient. If you are a self-advocate, remember that there could possibly be situations where it would be more beneficial for you to seek help from, and accept assistance from, a competent advocate. Having someone there who knows and understands your wishes will help ease your anxiety.

NANCY McCLELLAN & TASI McCLELLAN

22

BE PREPARED AND INFORMED

If you are the patient and your own advocate, or an advocate on behalf of a friend, family member, or loved one, BE PREPARED. Being prepared before you are in the hospital, or even sick, would be ideal, but unfortunately that is not always the case. As you study and read this book, start now by using it as an aid. Don't just read this book, use it!

Keep a small notebook and pen with you at all times. Write down all doctors' names, their specialty, and phone numbers. If you have their business card with you, keep it in your notebook. Know the nurses' names and write them down, you might need to call if the patient's condition changes, you have a question, or need other assistance. To help you in this endeavor, Appendix A has a "Daily Log" template to help you easily record this information. Have the patient's social security number and insurance information. The social security number and insurance information is needed at initial admittance and usually not needed again. Have with you a list of all current medications taken at home, both prescriptions and over-the-counter medications. List any supplements being taken, as well as the dosage and frequency with which they have been taking them. Have with you a list of allergies, if any. This would include allergies from medication, (i.e. aspirin, codeine), and environmental allergies (i.e., milk products, meats, chocolate). If the patient has advance care directives, have a copy with you and make sure that it is on their medical chart. Keep all telephone numbers of relatives, friends and any others you might need in a notebook, including your own home phone number (you would be surprised at what you forget in a crisis). Write down the hospital's phone number, the patient's current room number, and the direct phone number into the room.

A patient information sheet is provided at the back of this book for ease of recording relevant and important information discussed in this section (Appendix C – Patient Information Sheet and Patient Network Information Sheet).

As the advocate, you are the individual that should be the

information gatherer, as well as the one that will pass on information. If you are acting as the advocate for yourself, this certainly makes it more challenging. If there are many family members to contact, it is best to create some type of networking system. This ensures that you as the advocate or patient are not overwhelmed with concerned family, friends and loved ones. As the advocate, between helping the patient and being there for additional needs, having a networking system will help you to not be overwhelmed. I left updates on my mother's answering machine so I would not have to spend each evening calling all her friends.

Nurses will not tell anyone that is not family (or has appropriate legal rights) the status of the patient. You have the right to expect privacy in conversation and that your medical records will be kept confidential. No one has a right to your medical records without written consent unless they are an immediate medical caregiver. This means you can also make decisions around restricting what information may be communicated to anyone else.

There should be an advocate or an individual who has medical power of attorney. An individual family member, or advocate, should speak with the physicians and other medical care workers. Even if there are several family members that all have an equal right in the future care of the individual, you need only one family member who relays information between the medical personnel and the family. Thus you avoid information overlaps, repetitive conversations with health care personnel and possible conflicting information spoken to the RN or doctor and vice versa.

Cell phones are wonderful! As a patient advocate, being confined to a hospital bedside can be an isolating experience. Having the tools and ability to contact others is a great aid in not only time, but also security. In most hospitals cell phones are not allowed to be used in the building. There should be designated areas within the hospital and outside that you can use them. This is to ensure prevention of any potential interference with medical equipment, such as monitors and life support machines. Respect these rules, as you wouldn't want to unknowingly compromise anyone else's care.

If you are in a town or state that is not your home area you should have someone that you can call if you have a problem, such as car trouble, or need local assistance from an outside source. My home was in another state, but I knew my mother's close friends. I had the home phone number and cell phone number of a gentleman and his wife who had looked after my mother after my stepfather had died. These good people were my backup and the people I called in a problem situation. Several of my children lived about an hour away, so it was reassuring having multiple contacts that I could call locally.

More and more people are obtaining knowledge and information with access to the Internet, books, clinical education pamphlets, and support and awareness programs. Obtain information on the hospital, doctors, and other health care workers that care for you. See how the hospital, doctors, and auxiliaries measure up to your needs and expectations. Find out all you can about the latest medical discoveries and all the different options of medical care. Become familiar with family history and any medical conditions that may be inherited or environmentally caused. Ask the nurse or physician about any procedures or diseases that apply to your situation. They or the hospital will have information and pamphlets as well as possible support groups that you can contact after your hospital stay.

Find out about the hospital and their credentials. A reference that you can look for is the approval of the Joint Commission on Accreditation of Heath Care Organizations (JCAHO), or the Joint Commission on the Accreditation of Hospitals (JCAH). They set the standards for all hospitals. Not all hospitals are JCAH accredited, but a good majority are. Once every two years they score hospitals and make sure they meet the minimum standards.

When a doctor or nurse comes in to provide care for you or the patient, have a note pad in plain sight. This will remind you of the questions you may have thought about earlier which you should record on the pad as they come to you. The pad also provides a place to write the answers to the questions and any other questions that you might think of while talking with the medical personnel. My mother's doctors were in and out of the room within five minutes or less. When looking for answers, these precious moments can go by very quickly and it can be hours before you see them again, so you must be prepared.

In summary, it is important that you have prepared yourself with the following information and tools (this information is presented in checklist form in Appendix B):

NOTE BOOK
PEN/PENCIL
ALL AT HOME MEDICATIONS/SUPPLEMENTS BEING
    TAKEN
ANY ALLERGIES
DOCTOR'S NAMES, FIELD OF PRACTRICE AND
    PHONE NUMBERS
SOCIAL SECURITY NUMBER AND
    INSURANCE INFORMATION
LOVED ONE'S TELEPHONE NUMBERS
ADVANCE DIRECTIVES

As you experience the advocate role, you will learn that there is much you can do to protect the patient and ensure quality care.

DUTIES OF AN ADVOCATE OUTSIDE OF THE HOSPITAL

There is more stress for the patient than just fighting an illness or recovering from surgery during a hospital stay. Advocates have another duty besides what goes on at the hospital, and that is what is happening at the patient's place of residence. Reassurance and knowledge that every needful thing at the residence is being addressed gives the patient much needed peace of mind. Some simple things to keep in mind are:

Feed animals
Get mail
Pay bills
Water house plants and gardens
Yard care
Garbage pickup

If the patient is an independent or very private person, allow them to still have and exercise their own rights as much as possible. Take the mail to their room, so they can open it. If it is a long-term hospital stay and bills need to be paid, assist them as needed. Allow them to be involved in the everyday life as they once knew it, according to their ability and their desire. This can help accelerate a desire and willingness to work towards being able to return home.

As much as loved ones and friends want to come and visit or call – do your best to limit it! It is very draining on someone that is sick; they need their rest without any additional stress or interruptions. Consider the hospital's daily routine with family, friends, doctors, nurses, respiratory treatments, test, meals, phlebotomy, bathroom visits, IV changes, etc. Needless to say it is an active, busy day that can be very hectic. Be respectful and considerate whether you are a visitor or an advocate. That isn't to say that close friends and family can't be a positive influence on recovery, but a balance should be struck to ensure the well being of the patient.

WORKING WITH MEDICAL PROFESSIONALS

After complications with the first attempt to do my mother's hip surgery, the surgery was stopped and put on hold until she received a pacemaker to stabilize her heart rate. Two weeks after the pacemaker surgery, my mother had her hip surgery. Her care team included an RN, LPN, CNA and a physical therapist. I made an effort to know them and especially took time with the RN's that took care of her. Her recovery went well for the first four or five days. I noticed her declining physically and mentioned this concern to her primary care physician who dismissed my concern. I then went to the nurse who had been caring for her the last several days, because I knew my mother was in a definite decline. The nurse felt comfortable with me and revealed a concern that all the nurses had for my mother. Her decline seemed directly related to her blood pressure medication. I thanked her for the information and told her I would not mention the conversation. I immediately requested that a heart specialist (cardiologist) be called from the group that she had been seeing since her first bypass surgery. The doctor came within the hour, adjusted her blood pressure medications, and by the next morning my mother was alert and began the recovery process in earnest.

The nurse could be censored for doing this, but remember they are the ones that monitor the patient on a continuous basis, whereas the doctors are in and out. Nurse patient assignments have greatly increased these days, which limits their time with each patient and contributes to lower quality health care. After most patients were settled for the night, I learned that the night nurse had more time for questions and could provide more detailed information. Nurses are truly angels among us and are for most part dedicated caregivers. The registered nurse is your best ally and the patient's best ally. The nurse has all the medical information on the patient and all the information from conversations with the doctors. They also see the patient more often and for longer periods of time than any other medical personnel. Treat nurses with respect and friendliness, and take time to get acquainted. This incident was one of two times it was the observation and alertness of a qualified, caring nurse that saved my mother's life during the recovery stay in the hospital. Besides the physicians and the orders they give, your RN has ultimate responsibility for the patient.

You or your legal advocate have the right to know all the medical facts as well as request a consultation with all doctors. Often we are just given what is to be done, without discussion about alternatives, advantages and disadvantages. What about the patient's preferences? Doctors should initiate the discussion as to needed treatments and/

or procedures. Asking in-depth questions will empower you with better information, which allows you to make better decisions. When one has a clear understanding of all the facts related to the patient's medical crisis or situation, the results involving treatment and procedure can then have the best possible outcome. Some typical questions to ask the doctor might be:

> About the test, or procedure
> What happens?
> What will it show us?
> What can we learn from the test?
> Are other options or procedures available?
> What are the advantages and disadvantages?
> What are the likely long-term outcomes?

These questions and answers should give a clearer picture of the medical situation. Medical treatment is then determined jointly with the doctor and patient/advocate. If in doubt or confused, seek out a consultation meeting with all doctors that are involved in the patient's care. Do not be afraid to do this if you believe it is in the best interest of the patient.

Health care is big business and involves big money. In many situations insurance companies are now in charge. A doctor's need for a certain test for a patient is not always the final word.

Don't hesitate to ask questions or voice your concerns — often if needed. Also you may ask for another doctor's opinion if you feel uncertain or uneasy. Doctors, nurses, and other health care workers are not all knowing! They do make mistakes. Don't hesitate to question the situation if it doesn't seem right. It is not disrespectful if handled tactfully. It could save a lot of pain and suffering, or even someone's life!

It has been determined that a patient who is informed responds better in the hospital and to their medical treatments. For this to happen, you or your advocate must keep an open dialogue with your doctor or doctors and perpetuate mutual understanding in the medical treatment decision making process.

Have bedside manners! If a doctor is talking to you as the advocate, and your loved one is present, include the patient in the conversation. The doctor may directly speak to you, because you may be the one making the decisions for the individual, but make sure you include them in the conversation. Even if the patient does not understand completely, allow them to feel included and discuss what was decided after the doctor leaves. It is imperative the patient feel involved as much as possible whenever possible.

Most experienced medical personnel have great insight and knowledge as to what is happening to the patient. Medical personnel other than doctors (RN, CNA, RRT, etc.) are not allowed to interpret the information they are gathering. They are not allowed to diagnose based on the information. They complete the order that the doctors give them and/or gather information. These medical professionals can reiterate, treat, and discuss within the treatment and diagnosis realm as the doctor has determined. Some medical personnel are very knowledgeable and have a great depth of experience. Rely on these individuals for information — it can be a great aid in gaining valuable insight.

You should know those individuals that will be caring for the patient in the hospital situation. This includes those outside the medical field. For example, the people who deliver the food or clean the room. Be friendly and express appreciation for their service.

CHAPTER II
ADMISSION TO A HOSPITAL

BEING ADMITTED TO THE HOSPITAL

In most cases, you are likely to be admitted to the hospital without your advocate present, or you, as the advocate, will arrive after admission has taken place. As such, it is important as the patient to be prepared for this circumstance. As one is subjected to a lot of unknowns, being admitted to a hospital can be very scary, which in turn can cause a lot of unnecessary anxiety. Try to remember to relax and know that everyone is there to help you. Being admitted to a hospital can be done either through an emergency department, a doctor's direct admit through the doctor's office, or a scheduled surgery or procedure.

Bring a notebook with you. Pay special attention to having the list of medications you are presently taking. List the name, dose and frequency. Make sure you have identification with you as well as your insurance card information, social security number, and a list of any known allergies.

Being admitted to the hospital means lots and lots of paperwork. If you are being directly admitted to the hospital by a doctors office and/or having last minute surgery you will be directed to an admissions office, where they will admit you and take you to your designated area. If you have a pre-scheduled surgery you would have already done pre-admission paperwork at home, and your physician should have given you that information to take care of before you even reach the hospital. In many hospitals, and depending on how quickly they have to admit you based on your medical needs, a secretary will come around and confirm all the paperwork is properly filled out, insurance cards are copied, and billing information recorded.

Secure your personal items. After using all of your identifications, insurance cards, social security card, etc., have your advocate, loved one, or friend, take your valuables home. You will not need them again. Never leave any personal belongings, such as a purse, cell phone, or anything else of value in the room or bedside. If you are your own advocate, speak with the nurse and ask for your personal belongings to be locked up. Don't just give them to him or her. Normally a hospital security guard will come to your room where he or she will fill out paperwork accounting for your personal belongings. Then they will take your belongings to a secure place to be locked up.

ENTERING THROUGH THE EMERGENCY ROOM

Emergency departments are getting busier and busier. Nationally there have been many closures of emergency departments. People are living longer than ever before. This increase in life expectancy and closures of emergency departments is causing an increase in the number of people seen on an emergency basis.

There are two ways to enter the emergency room:
—Walking in
—Via ambulance

Walking in you will be asked to fill out paperwork and be seen by a triage registered nurse to determine the severity of your condition. At that time you will either be seen immediately by another nurse and a physician, or will have to wait in the waiting room for the next emergency room bed available. When there are a lot of patients in the emergency room you may have to wait a while. If during this wait your condition changes from when you first entered the emergency room and were seen by the nurse (for example, you begin feeling faint, having chest pain, massive bleeding, an increase in difficulty in breathing, excruciating headache, etc.) and you have been asked to continue to wait, DON'T! Insist on being seen at once. In cases where the advocate is present, they should pay close attention to any of these changes in the patient's condition.

Upon arrival to the hospital in an ambulance, you will be taken immediately in for care. Depending on your stability you will be seen by a doctor immediately, or soon thereafter. There will be a secretary that will come to you and have you fill out forms for care to be given, as well as recording insurance and billing information.

In the emergency room you will be evaluated and treated. It will be determined if you will be admitted to the hospital, or sent home with instructions to follow up with your general practitioner. If your medical condition deems that more testing, treatment, or monitoring needs to be done you will be admitted to the hospital. You will be taken to a specific floor according to your medical needs.

BEING ADMITTED BY A DOCTOR'S DIRECT ADMIT

Being admitted by a direct admit means for example, you were just at the doctor's office, or have contacted your doctor and he has told you to go to the hospital to be admitted. The admitting doctor will have contacted the hospital to tell them you are coming and the initial care he or she wishes to start you on will take place until further evaluation can be done.

Being directly admitted to the hospital, you will go directly to admittance office or emergency room depending on the time of day and hospital policy. There the admittance staff will help you do the necessary paperwork and take you to your room. When you reach the designated room, your assigned nurse will assist you from there.

As stated before, make sure you know the current medication that you have been taking and dosage. Take your physicians name and number, personal identification and insurance information. Don't assume that your doctor will know your current medications; they see many patients and chances are they will need to be refreshed as to the medications you are currently on. Having the worksheet filled out with allergies and medications as previously discussed will aid you greatly.

SCHEDULED SURGERY or PROCEDURES

Hospitals are getting a greater amount of money for outpatient procedures and care. Because of this, there is a greater number of procedures done on an outpatient basis.

On the day of your scheduled surgery you will need to follow the instructions that your doctor's office has given you as to where to go, when to go, and what preparation is necessary. It is a good idea to double-check with your physician as to what medications you can take before your surgery.

If you are pre-registered, go to the admittance office, same-day surgery front desk, or registration office for final paperwork; from there they will take you to the designated waiting area prior to any procedure. The nurse will have you undress and gown according to the needs of the procedure. You may be asked to remove dentures, glasses or contacts, and all jewelry, with the exception of your wedding ring, which they will usually securely tape to your finger. These items will be placed in a secure place, and given back to you after the procedure. It is ultimately the best thing not to bring items such as jewelry and other personal items to the hospital. The nurse will finish up any paperwork and ask you questions such as:

> Last medications taken? How much?
> Last time you ate or drank?
> How tall you are?
> How much do you weigh?

The nurse will take your blood pressure, temperature, and complete other initial preparations. For a same-day surgery or procedure, an anesthesiologist should come and speak with you prior. If you were already admitted and in the hospital and had a scheduled surgery, the anesthesiologist will usually see you in your hospital room the day/evening prior to the surgery. If you have any questions for the anesthesiologist be sure to ask them then.

After your surgery, you will usually wake up in a post-operations room where you will be monitored for any problems with coming out of the anesthesia. Usually the doctor will come and speak to you, after which, you will be transferred either back to your room, a surgical nursing floor, or discharged to go home. Your loved one or advocate will be notified that the surgery has been completed. Before you leave the hospital make sure you ask when can you restart your medications.

Never hesitate to ask any questions. Before and after the procedure the nurses will be happy to answer any questions or concerns you may have. You usually will not be able to drive yourself home after most procedures, so make sure you have someone there for you.

CHAPTER III
KNOWING YOUR RIGHTS

THE PATIENT'S BILL OF RIGHTS

Adopted by many hospitals, The American Hospital Association (AHA) has set standards and rights that you as a patient should have in a medical crisis. You should become aware and understand what your rights are. Throughout the rest of the book we will elaborate on many of these rights.

A Patient's Bill of Rights

Reprinted with permission of the American Hospital Association, copyright 1992.

A Patient's Bill of Rights was first adopted by the American Hospital Association in 1973.

This revision was approved by the AHA Board of Trustees on October 21, 1992.

Introduction: Effective health care requires collaboration between patients and physicians and other health care professionals.

Open and honest communication, respect for personal and professional values, and sensitivity to differences are integral to optimal patient care. As the setting for the provision of health services, hospitals must provide a foundation for understanding and respecting the rights and responsibilities of patients, their families, physicians, and other caregivers. Hospitals must ensure a health care ethic that respects the role of patients in decision-making about treatment choices and other aspects of their care. Hospitals must be sensitive to cultural, racial, linguistic, religious, age, gender, and other differences as well as the needs of persons with disabilities.

The American Hospital Association presents A Patient's Bill of Rights with the expectation that it will contribute to more effective patient care and be supported by the hospital on behalf of the institution, its medical staff, employees, and patients. The American Hospital Association encourages health care institutions to tailor this bill of rights to their patient community by translating and/or simplifying the language of this bill of rights as may be necessary to ensure that patients and their families understand their rights and responsibilities.

Bill of Rights

These rights can be exercised on the patient's behalf by a designated surrogate or proxy decision maker if the patient lacks decision-making capacity, is legally incompetent, or is a minor.

1. The patient has the right to considerate and respectful care.

2. The patient has the right to and is encouraged to obtain from physicians and other direct caregivers relevant, current, and understandable information concerning diagnosis, treatment, and prognosis.

Except in emergencies when the patient lacks decision-making capacity and the need for treatment is urgent, the patient is entitled to the opportunity to discuss and request information related to the specific procedures and/or treatments, the risks involved, the possible length of recuperation, and the medically reasonable alternatives and their accompanying risks and benefits.

Patients have the right to know the identity of physicians, nurses, and others involved in their care, as well as when those involved are students, residents, or other trainees. The patient also has the right to know the immediate and long-term financial implications of treatment choices, insofar as they are known.

3.   The patient has the right to make decisions about the plan of care prior to and during the course of treatment and to refuse a recommended treatment or plan of care to the extent permitted by law and hospital policy and to be informed of the medical consequences of this action. In case of such refusal, the patient is entitled to other appropriate care and services that the hospital provides or transfer to another hospital. The hospital should notify patients of any policy that might affect patient choice within the institution.

4.   The patient has the right to have an advance directive (such as a living will, health care proxy, or durable power of attorney for health care) concerning treatment or designating a surrogate decision maker with the expectation that the hospital will honor the intent of that directive to the extent permitted by law and hospital policy.

Health care institutions must advise patients of their rights under state law and hospital policy to make informed medical choices, ask if the patient has an advance directive, and include that information in patient records. The patient has the right to timely information about hospital policy that may limit its ability to implement fully a legally valid advance directive.

5.   The patient has the right to every consideration of privacy. Case discussion, consultation, examination, and treatment should be conducted so as to protect each patient's privacy.

6.The patient has the right to expect that all communications and records pertaining to his/her care will be treated as confidential by the hospital, except in cases such as suspected abuse and public health hazards when reporting is permitted or required by law. The patient has the right to expect that the hospital will emphasize the confidentiality of this information when it releases it to any other parties entitled to review information in these records.

7.   The patient has the right to review the records pertaining to his/her medical care and to have the information explained or interpreted as necessary, except when restricted by law.

8.   The patient has the right to expect that, within its capacity and policies, a hospital will make reasonable response to the request of a patient for appropriate and medically indicated care and services. The hospital must provide evaluation, service, and/or referral as indicated by the urgency of the case. When medically appropriate and legally permissible, or when a patient has so requested, a patient may be transferred to another facility. The institution to which the patient is to be transferred must first have accepted the patient for transfer. The patient must also have the benefit of complete information and explanation concerning the need for, risks, benefits, and alternatives to such a transfer.

9.   The patient has the right to ask and be informed of the existence of business relationships among the hospital, educational institutions, other health care providers, or payers that may influence the patient's treatment and care.

10.   The patient has the right to consent to or decline to participate in proposed research studies or human experimentation affecting care and treatment or requiring direct patient involvement, and to have those studies fully explained prior to consent. A patient who declines to participate in research or experimentation is entitled to the most effective care that the hospital can otherwise provide.

11. The patient has the right to expect reasonable continuity of care when appropriate and to be informed by physicians and other caregivers of available and realistic patient care options when hospital care is no longer appropriate.

12. The patient has the right to be informed of hospital policies and practices that relate to patient care, treatment, and responsibilities. The patient has the right to be informed of available resources for resolving disputes, grievances, and conflicts, such as ethics committees, patient representatives, or other mechanisms available in the institution. The patient has the right to be informed of the hospital's charges for services and available payment methods.

The collaborative nature of health care requires that patients, or their families/surrogates, participate in their care. The effectiveness of care and patient satisfaction with the course of treatment depend, in part, on the patient fulfilling certain responsibilities. Patients are responsible for providing information about past illnesses, hospitalizations, medications, and other matters related to health status. To participate effectively in decision making, patients must be encouraged to take responsibility for requesting additional information or clarification about their health status or treatment when they do not fully understand information and instructions. Patients are also responsible for ensuring that the health care institution has a copy of their written advance directive if they have one. Patients are responsible for informing their physicians and other caregivers if they anticipate problems in following prescribed treatment.

Patients should also be aware of the hospital's obligation to be reasonably efficient and equitable in providing care to other patients and the community. The hospital's rules and regulations are designed to help the hospital meet this obligation. Patients and their families are responsible for making reasonable accommodations to the needs of the hospital, other patients, medical staff, and hospital employees.

Patients are responsible for providing necessary information for insurance claims and for working with the hospital to make payment arrangements, when necessary.

A person's health depends on much more than health care services. Patients are responsible for recognizing the impact of their life-style on their personal health.

Conclusion

Hospitals have many functions to perform, including the enhancement of health status, health promotion, and the prevention and treatment of injury and disease; the immediate and ongoing care and rehabilitation of patients; the education of health professionals, patients, and the community; and research. All these activities must be conducted with an overriding concern for the values and dignity of patients.

CHAPTER IV
HOSPITAL EXPERIENCE

THE HOSPITAL EXPERIENCE

When one is thrust into the hospital experience, being informed, prepared and aware will lower the stress in this uncomfortable environment and give you more control.

FAMILIARIZE YOURSELF WITH HOSPITAL POLICES AND AREAS

Depending on the hospital area that the patient is in, there will be different rules and policies that you will need to be aware of. Be informed and follow them. They exist for a reason. Every area has different guidelines, some of which include:

> Visiting hours
> Ages of children allowed to visit
> Various personal items the can or cannot be brought in (For
>   example: no flowers or outside food in Intensive

Care Unit (ICU) rooms.)
Isolation rooms, meaning you may have to wear protective
    clothing.
Limiting visitations to high risk patients

Check with the nurse if you want to bring in any personal items such as radios, hair dryers, medical equipment, or anything that uses electricity. The item or items may need to be approved before using them at the hospital in order to ensure they don't cause interference with any medical equipment.

Be aware of your surroundings. If you are pregnant, or have a suppressed immune system, there are rooms that you should not be in, even if your loved one is rooming with someone else. It may not affect him or her, but it could affect you. For example, someone on chemotherapy may expose you to radiation; or someone with certain dangerous viruses can potentially expose you. Patients that pose a potential problem to others are usually in isolation rooms, but be aware of your surrounding and make sure you protect yourself. Precautions are usually posted on the door or near the patient when appropriate. Don't be afraid to ask the nurse if you are concerned or have questions as to what precautions should be taken.

MEDICAL FLOORS

There are many medical floors in a hospital, all to serve specific conditions and medical needs. Be aware that each hospital has a different way of labeling these areas. For example, one hospital may call a floor that you would usually transfer to after being in an intensive care unit (ICU) an intermediate care unit (IMC). Another hospital may call this same unit a progressive care unit (PCU). Don't be confused by the labels they place on certain floors.

The different floors have specialized registered nurses, monitors, and various caregivers to provide for given diagnosis and medical needs. The patient will be monitored according to the critical needs of their status.

Changing rooms happens frequently for numerous reasons, such as:

Patient to Registered Nurse ratio

Isolation precautions

Special needs

Again, as previously mentioned, have your networking system in place so you as the advocate can let them know of these changes. That way if someone shows up and the person is not there, it will not cause undue concern.

Below is a list of typical floors and units that you may find in your hospital:

Burn Center—Severely burned patients

CCU—Cardiac Care Unit (heart patients)

Geriatric floor— Caring for patients that are older

ICU—Intensive Care Unit (critical patients)

IMC or PCU—Intermediate Care; or Progressive Care Units-next step after ICU

Medical—Medical floor

NICU or ISCU— Newborn Intensive Care Unit or Intensive Special Care Unit— Premature babies or newborns with congenitive abnormalities)

Oncology— Floors for patients with tumors

Orthopedics— Joint, muscle, ligament, and cartilage disorders

PACU— Post and/or Pre-Anesthesiology room (prep and/or recovery room from surgery or procedures)

Pediatrics— Children aged from a few days old to 16.

Surgical— Patients recovering form surgery

TCU— Transitional Care Unit; Place to stay between hospital and nursing facilities.

IDENTIFYING STAFF MEMBERS

All employees should be wearing some type of identification badge displayed where you can see it. It should tell you their name, department, and title. If you have any question as to who someone is, ask! You have a right to know who is coming in contact with the patient. Individuals must tell you who they are, and what department they are associated with. All hospital staff, from security workers, x-ray technicians, and lab workers, to those that clean the room, should be wearing visible identification.

WHO'S WHO?

It quickly becomes confusing when you have many physicians, nurses, nursing assistants, respiratory therapists, phlebotomists and the like all coming and going. The list of medical professionals you come into contact with can grow very quickly. All these individuals are gathering information and performing duties to help the patient. These tests and procedures all come from a physician's order. The question then becomes: Which physician, and why? You can see many physicians during the course of a day. It is required that your ordering physician, primary care doctor, or anyone that has you under their direct care, see you once every 24 hours. If you have been, or are being seen by a specialist, they will follow up while you are under their care. As an advocate, be aware of the physicians and what they order. If something doesn't seem right you have the right to question it and as the advocate you should question it.

You can have many doctors interacting with the patient, and individually they won't know everything. After seeing their patients, physicians will write notes on the patient's chart. They will identify their observations and findings and make notes as to the course of care they wish to pursue. In one section of your chart they write orders that are to be done: tests, procedures, medication, or other various actions. In another section the doctor writes "progressive notes" as to their findings and plan of care. When the next physician comes to do his/her evaluation, they read what the last physician has summarized and continue on with their care for the patient. In some cases this is the only communication these physicians have with each other. More and more patients have several chronic diseases, causing more physician specialists caring for one patient. These physicians spend a lot of time coordinating the care. It is very time consuming, but must be done carefully in order to ensure an aggregated course of care is establish for the patient.

Make your own physician chart, putting the primary care physician at the top and then add the specialty doctors as they enter the patient's medical situation. Put the doctor's name, phone number, specialty and reason for their services.

It is easy to see how complicated it can become when many specialty doctors are needed. As an advocate you should have one doctor make sure all the medical aspects are being correlated. Not just the specifics of one specialty. These doctors usually work well together. But it is really important that one physician is making sure the big picture is being evaluated as well as the critical details. In doing so, simple issues will hopefully not be overlooked. For example, medication given by one physician could have a negative impact on the treatment being prescribed by another physician. It is very important that all of the functions are being double-checked and care is being given to the patient that is in their best interests.

As an advocate you can make sure that day after day these doctors are coordinating care, especially if the patient's original doctor is not there, and a partner of the original doctor is seeing you. Many partners don't want to make final decisions, because they are not familiar with the patient's entire history. If you get a few days of that in a row, it becomes very frustrating and progress can be significantly hindered.

In the case of special procedures or surgery, doctors do try to consult other caring physicians before and after the surgery. As an advocate, make sure you ask exactly whom they have talked to before the procedure. The physician ordering the procedure or surgery needs to be aware of the patient's full history, as well as be mindful of their wishes. Make sure they see the full picture and don't simply chalk them up as just another patient or just another test. By all means, the patient is not a number! It is their life!

It sometimes seems strange the doctor you go to at the doctors office doesn't see you in the hospital. In some situations, PCPs (primary care physician) or GPs (general practitioner) are not taking care of their patients in the hospital. Many are giving up their hospital rights and just allowing a hospitalist (a physician specializing in the care of hospitalized patients) to assume responsibility over their patients while they are in the hospital. When you are released from the hospital you will return back to seeing your normal PCP. This has its pros and cons. If you have a hospiatalist caring for you, pay special attention to the patient's medical history and needs to be sure they are addressed. They will not know the patient as well as the PCP/GP.

Here is a list of some medical professionals you may come in contact with during hospitalization:

Anesthesiologist - Physician specializing in anesthetics

Board Certified Specialist -Those that voluntary take vigorous tests in a particular medical specialty. These individuals have gone beyond standard requirements for licensure. You can find out if a physician is board certified by obtaining through a public or hospital library, the Official ABMS Directory of Board Certified Medical Specialists.

Cardiologist - Specialist of heart diseases and coronary arteries.

Dermatologist - Specialist of skin and its diseases.

Doctor of Osteopathy (D.O) M.D - Use of osteopathic techniques to prevent, treat, and diagnosis diseases.

Endocrinologist - Specialist in gland and duct disorders.

Gastroenteroligist - Specialist of the stomach, intestine, esophagus, liver, gallbladder, and pancreas.

Geriatrician - Board Certified Physician works with elderly patients.

Gynecologist - Specialist in female reproductive system

Hematologist - Specialist of blood and disorders.

Medical Doctor (MD)-Doctor of Medicine, diagnoses and treats patients. State Licensure.

Nephrologist - Specialist in the function and diseases of kidneys.

Neurologist - Nervous system specialist

Oncologist - Tumor specialist

Ophthalmologist - Disorders of the eye

Orthopedist - Specialists in bone, muscles, and joint disorders

Osteologist - Specialist of the bones

Otolaryngologist - An ears, nose and throat specialist

Pharmacist - Specialist that knows drug actions and side effects as well as controls the dispensing of drugs.

Primary Care Physician (PCP)- Specialist in family care or pediatrics.

Proctologist - Specialist in disorders and diseases of the anus, rectum, and colon

Pulmonologist - Specialist in disorders of the lung and chest

Radiologist - Specialist using x-ray or other sources of radiation for diagnosis

Rehabilitation Specialist - Specialist in correcting injury disabilities

Resident (use to be called an Internist)- A training period after graduating from four years of a college or university and four years of medical school. Residency is usually 3-7 years.

Rheumatologist - Specialist in rheumatism and arthritis

Specialists - After normal residency of 3-7 years, specialist take an additional 1-3 years for additional specialty requirements.

Surgeon - Specialist in diagnosing, treating, and repair injuries and deformities by surgery

Urologist - Specialist in urinary tracts of both sexes, and in the male reproductive system

●

SPECIAL PROCEDURES

Below is a short list of some very routine procedures that many patients have. Realize that some of these procedures can be done at bedside, and others may have to be performed somewhere else within the hospital. These procedures are all ordered by you doctor and are just a handful of tests and/or procedures that one may go through during their entire hospital stay:

Arterial blood gas (ABG) - Blood taken from an artery shows blood PH, oxygenation, CO2 (carbon dioxide) and some kidney functions.

Biopsy – Obtaining a tissue sample for evaluation.

Computerized Tomography (CT scan) - Radiation beam creating images that a computer interpolates.

Dialysis -The process of removing blood from a patient whose kidney functions are faulty, using a machine that provides a means for removing certain undesirable substances from the blood, or of adding needed components to it.

Echocardiogram – Records the motion of the heart via ultrasound.

Electrocardiogram (EKG or ECG) - measures electrical activity of the heart.

Electroencephalogram (EEG) - a tracing of electrical activity of the brain.

Electromyogram (EMG) - Surface electrode placed to measure electrical signals of skeletal muscles and nerves.

Exercise stress test (EST) - measures heart and lung functions

Lab work - usually performed by a phlebotomist who takes blood from veins. This is usually done in the early morning hours so the result will be back when the doctor shows up that day.

Magnetic Resonance Imaging (MRI) - A magnetic field with radio frequency waves creates images for evaluation.

Oncology procedures - treats tumors through either

chemotherapy or radiation

Oscopy - visualize with a scope. (Laryngoscopy- scope the larynx, Colonoscopy- scope the colon)

Pulmonary Function Test (PFT) - uses a spirometer to determine measurements of large and small airways (of the lungs).

Radioisotope Scans - these include brain, bone, lung, thyroid, and liver scans. A radioactive substance is given through an IV and then pictures are taken to see the uptake of the radioactive materials, creating images for interpretation.

Roentgenogram (x-rays) - Radioactive waves create images.

Sonogram (ultrasound) - High frequency waves to create vibrations off of soft tissues. The vibration (echo) is translated into images and pictures to be interpreted.

IN HOSPITAL INFECTIONS

Infections are alive and well in the hospital environment, but precautions can be taken using basic common sense. My mother received her many pills as the nurse picked them out of the pill cup and placed them in her mouth. At the time it didn't register with me, that this exchange could be more then just pills passing from nurse to patient. Why didn't I request that the nurse wear gloves or wash her hands before administering her medications? A majority of the nurses never did this either. Making this request isn't rude, it is practicing practical safety precautions.

The Center for Disease Control and Prevention (CDC), and the Occupational Safety and Health Administration (OSHA), work together in protecting, educating, and standardizing safety polices throughout hospitals. All hospital professionals are required to follow precautionary policies because of the way viruses and diseases are spread.

The precautions are categorized according to the way the diseases are spread:

Airborne Precautions: Transmitted by airborne droplets evaporated in the air.

Contact Precautions: Transmitted by direct contact (skin to skin), or indirect (obtained off surfaces previously touched by the patient)

Droplet Precautions: Droplets transmitted by talking, sneezing, and/or coughing

Universal Precautions: Transmitted by bodily fluids (blood, vomit, saliva, and urine)

Following precautionary measures can help ensure your protection as well as help protect those around you. It can't be emphasized enough that you, as a patient or advocate, follow the universal precaution policy while in the hospital, especially if any of these circumstances apply:

A child under the age of 5

A depressed or compromised immune system

An elderly person

This precaution states that hand washing is a must. When touching blood or body fluids you need to wear gloves and appropriate apparel. Encourage correct placement and disposal of needles; don't let the nurse leave needles on the bed. This requirement is not only smart, but can be a life-saving, simple task. As an advocate you can encourage these standards, and use them as well. Wash your hands both coming and going! If you are sick, be courteous to the patient and don't visit them. If you must visit them while sick, ask the nurse for a mask and wash your hands. This not only helps protect the patient you may be concerned with, but other patients that may share a room with them.

If you are in an isolation room, a critical care unit, or other designated area where there are specific guidelines, you will need to follow them. The nurse will explain what is required of you. Some type of reminder will usually be posted next to the patient's room. This is to remind and specify actions that need to be taken not only by you, but anyone who is to come in contact with the patient.

Being in an isolation room doesn't necessary mean that you will catch something from the patient. It could also be a reverse isolation room, where the patient is sensitive to outside elements due to a suppressed immune system and therefore they are at high risk to any exposure.

Nosocomial infections are infections that are passed on within the hospital. This is actually a big problem! These infections can be acquired via transfer from:

> Patient to Staff
> Staff to Staff
> Staff to Patient.

Drug resistant diseases are a great concern as time goes on. Encourage a clean environment and good hand washing. If a care worker wears gloves while working with the patient, they shouldn't be offended — it is only for their benefit and the benefit of others. Encourage it!

VITALS

Numbers reveal how the patient is doing and are a window into what is happening in the body. The daily recordings of these numbers is significant. Numbers such as blood pressure, heart rate, oxygen saturation percentages, respiratory rate, temperature, and measurements of food and liquid intake and output can give you an indication of the patient's daily condition. Monitoring the numbers and writing them down is a good idea. Find out from the registered nurse what should be normal for the patient. What is acceptable or normal is different depending on age or condition. Also, you need to be aware the medication that the patient is being given will affect those numbers. That means if you are a number watcher, and are going to be concerned about them, pay special attention to the medication given, including dosages and frequency. For example, oxygen saturation versus the amount of oxygen the patient is on, or beta-blockers that will slow down the heart rate.

When I gave my mother's numbers to my daughter in-law, she gave me valuable insight into my mother's condition. A medical professional outside the hospital can be beneficial in helping you understand the vitals.

Vital signs consist not only of numbers, but also physical appearance and response, as well as overall patient disposition. Everyone reacts to drugs and medication differently; how the body responds will be shown not only by change in vitals, but also by the patient's physical appearance or the way they feel.

Doctors are positive and very optimistic, and this is how it should be. When I asked about my mother's declining or changing numbers (blood pressure, oxygen saturation, heart rate, respiratory rate), the answer was always the same. "She is eighty-two years old, and it is going to take time for her to recover." The problem I encountered with my mother's heart doctor's positive and optimistic attitude was that it was unfounded in our reality as I witnessed her slow demise. A problem that comes from doctors being too positive and optimistic is contradictory expectation set for recovery and the actual unfolding decline that the patient can exhibit.

In a reflective personal side note, the heart doctor who instigated the bypass surgery was very accommodating and attentive in the beginning, and then there were his lapses. He didn't observe my mother's complete medical care that included the specialty doctors and the cause and effect scenario on her that their individual treatments were inducing. The other lapses are not pertinent for the point I hope to make. It seemed obvious to me and several other individuals that visited my mother regularly that she was progressing backwards not forward, and it had nothing to do with her age. Maybe it was because we knew her so well, and how much she truly loved life. We had witnessed her determination and effort to recover quickly from past surgeries, and that passion was simply not there. My mother was not a quitter, as she had overcome many adversities throughout her life. She had learned how to overcome and move forward. Looking back, I believe she had really let go many weeks before her death. Once I stopped listening to the doctor and evaluated the whole picture, which included a sobering look at the realities of the situation, I too could let go and let my mother move on. I mention this only for your consideration. The doctors can't know the patient as you know the person. Even as the patient/advocate, you must exert your rights and even give information about yourself or the patient that you would not normally give, in order to influence the doctor's perception of the patient within the medical situation. If you are your own advocate, don't forget that this is happening to YOU! This will help ensure the doctors present you with the right options for your nature and personality.

NUTRITIONAL NEEDS

Calorie intake and nutritious foods are important when one is in a vulnerable physical condition and recovering from illness, surgery or injury. Everyone has different needs nutritionally. Any diet restrictions you may have, whether medical, religious, or personal, can be addressed. Make sure you tell the hospital of any known needs when you are admitted so they can arrange your menu selections.

My mother required some help with her meals, so it was important that someone was with her at mealtimes. Her appetite had never been great in the morning, so I didn't arrive for breakfast to help since she didn't eat much that early anyway. It was also one less meal with me nagging her to eat. The last two weeks before her death, I tried to be there for every meal, and the few times that I was taking care of family business, she had a close friend that would assist her. I did notice that she was never encouraged to drink after her IV's were disconnected, and I made an effort to encourage her water intake. Four years ago during the hip surgery recovery, the nurses and LPN's encouraged water intake every time they came in the room. This encouragement is very beneficial. Some medical conditions could require the opposite, so make sure you check with the doctor or nurse as to dietary habits that you should encourage.

I visited with mother's doctor because her calorie intake was so low. He said that I could bring her any food from outside the hospital, and also firmly admonished her about her need to eat. My mother had great respect for her doctors, and in each hospital situation tried her best to do what they wanted. In past hospital stays, she had maneuvered her release from the hospital early by complaining about the hospital food and not eating as well as needed, but enough to encourage improvement and gain sufficient strength. Initially I thought she was trying this again. When the food I brought in was refused and her efforts at eating were about the same, then I knew she would most likely never recover. This insight came during the third week of her ordeal.

Consulting with the patient and helping to fill out the daily menus as needed perpetuates meals and nutrition that are appealing for the patient. If the patient is not able to fill out daily menus for reasons such as medications, confusion, or any other reason, the hospital cafeteria will be happy to make the decision for you. Calorie intake might be low because the patient needs help eating. Hospital personnel are often too busy to do this needed service. Staffing is very limited and caregivers are stretched in their capacities. Because staffing is short it would be smart to have a loved one, family member, or friend stay and help with meals. Find out when breakfast, lunch and dinner are because the times may not be what you expect. For example, in my mother's hospital the mealtimes were as follows: Breakfast 7:30 a.m., Lunch 11:30 a.m., and Dinner 4:30 p.m.

A lot of patients could use help in opening packaged food and eating in general. If the patient is a youth or child it would be highly suggested to stay with them at all times during the meal. They just aren't likely to get the supervision that meets their needs. If you have an infant in NICU you will need to follow the policies outlined by the individual units.

With some patients, nurses may measure what food is eaten or what is expelled through urination. It is very important to not fill up the water pitcher or give the patient food from home without asking the nurse first. Simply consult with your RN before you give them any food or beverage. Two examples are: a diabetic, where they monitor their glucose levels, so bringing outside food to them may interfere with the medical care given; another example is a patient with congestive heart failure (CHF). They normally closely monitor the amount of fluid intake.

The hospital dietician (RD) is a valued resource. They encourage healthy eating and nutrition and ensure a nutritional balance to meet the needs of the patient. If you feel like your loved one is not eating enough, and it has been a few days and no one has addressed it, contact your doctor and request a dietician. They will make sure the nutritional needs are being met. This is very crucial to recovery. An example of what a dietician may help with: metabolic testing, which sees how much energy is being burned and ensures the patient is getting enough nutrition to allow their body to heal and become strong. They can also help by suggesting such things as thickening agents to help with patients that choke a lot while eating.

Before some surgeries or procedures you are not allowed to eat. If you have been told that, and you are still brought food, question it! Mistakes do happen. Be on top of that, and don't assume the hospital worker knows. Ask the registered nurse first. Also, a good advocate for a diabetic should check their tray to ensure there is nothing there that shouldn't be. As an advocate, don't let the lack of oversight complicate the situation.

The dietician recommended that my mother receive a nutritional boost drink with every meal and often this was about all that she would consume. There was a medical situation happening inside her that did not become clear until about the third week. The lack of calorie intake gave me a warning and prepared me for what later transpired. Remember to voice concerns to the doctor and dietician. They too want the patient to get strong and recover.

MEDICATIONS

In the world of medicine there seems to be a pill for everything. Keeping track of your medications and understanding them will give you greater insight and will empower you as an advocate.

Make sure your registered nurse and doctor know the medications that were being taken at home. The doctors may change the strength, dosage, or some medications completely so make sure they know exactly what was being taken. Keep in the mind that for the medications being taken, the medical personnel may not dispense it in the same form as it was being taken at home (for example, a pill may now being given through an IV). Make sure those medications are known and are being followed through with. Don't assume that it is on record, or the doctor will know. Doctors have many patients, and they can't be expected to remember all of the medications that a patient is receiving.

Leave any medication the patient may have been taking at home. No medications can be taken from home while you are in the hospital unless approved by the doctor. Taking medications from home can put the patient in danger, because the nurse can give them something that could have an adverse reaction with that medication. Ask what medications are being administered. The registered nurse should be able to tell you every time.

Find out what the normal range of dosage for a given drug is, and compare it to what is being given. If what is being given seems like a lot more than the normal dosage, question it! This could save a life! Patients and family members have the right to refuse any treatment or medication given.

KNOW YOUR DRUGS

The American Medical Association and *Reader's Digest* have categorized the medications into the categories listed below. It is beneficial to know these categories as you become familiar with medication you, or your loved one, will be given. This way you will have an idea what system the drug is working on. Keep in mind that most drugs have side effects, which could affect more than one bodily system. As an advocate, you can fill out the worksheets in Appendix D to help organize this information. The following are the segmented drug categories:

> Drugs and the central nervous system
> Drugs for digestive disorders
> Drugs for the heart and circulation
> Drugs for respiratory disorders
> Drugs for pain and inflammation
> Drugs for infections and infestations
> Drugs for hormonal disorders
> Anticancer drugs
> Drugs for eye, ear, and skin disorders

WARNINGS ABOUT MEDICATIONS

From the *Reader's Digest* article, "What To Ask Your Doctor!" 1991, page 52:
"Not everyone responds to drugs in the same way, and some people are particularly vulnerable to adverse effects of drugs. High-risk groups include:
> Elderly people
> Women who are pregnant or breast-feeding
> Babies and children
> People with liver disease
> People with kidney disease
> People who are taking certain other medications"

There are many side effects to medications, so make sure you understand them and are aware that those side effects can and do effect other functions of the body.

A couple of examples of side effects are medications such as opioids (Morphine, Oxycontin, Vicodin, Codeine and Darvocet) are constipation and decreased breathing. Respiratory inhalers such as Albuterol or Racemicepinephrine increase the heart rate. These are only a couple of the side effects for these given medications, but it gives you a idea what the effects can be.

The are also other complications that can be caused by medications. Be aware that these complications can exist:

> **Allergies** - Antigen/Antibodies fight against the drug
> **Disease-associated effects** - Your given disease may alter the medication or its function.
> **Drug Interaction** - Drugs interact with each other
> **Genetic** - Lack of enzymes or metabolic pathways
> **Intolerance** - Quantitatively greater effects at normal ranges.
> **Overdose** - To much given, or a decrease in metabolism.

There are key questions to ask your doctor about the medications you are taking. As outlined by the *Reader's Digest* book "Know Your Drug" and the American Medical Association, the following provides suggestions as to what you should ask your doctor:

"WHAT SHOULD I ASK MY DOCTOR?

Lack of information is one of the most common reasons for failing to take a drug properly. Other reasons include forgetfulness, fear of taking drugs, the cost of the drug, and side effects of and adverse reactions to a drug. Whenever your doctor writes a prescription for you, there are several things you should know. Some questions can be answered by reading the medication's label and package insert. However, feel free to ask your doctor any questions you have about your new medication.

HOW SOON WILL THE DRUG START WORKING?

If you do not know when you may start to feel the effects of the drug, you may think that the medication is not working and may be tempted to increase the dosage or stop taking the drug. This can be dangerous.

HOW SHOULD I TAKE THE DRUG?
This is important to know because different forms of drugs work differently. For example, you need to dissolve some types of tablets in your mouth rather than swallow them. If you do not take the medication correctly, it may not be effective, or it may even have an adverse effect.

DO I HAVE TO WAKE UP AT NIGHT TO TAKE MY MEDICATION?
Timing of doses influences the effectiveness of your medication. In most cases, 'once daily' can be at any time, but should be at about the same hour each day. 'Twice daily' means approximately every 12 hours. If 'four times a day' is specified, ask your doctor if you should wake up during the night to take your medicine.

CAN I TAKE ALL THREE OF MY MEDICATIONS AT THE SAME TIME?
If you are taking several different drugs, ask your doctor if you can take them at the same time, or if they must be taken several hours apart. Some drugs interfere with the absorption of others.

SHOULD I TAKE THE DRUG AFTER EATING?
Food and liquids can make some medications less effective by reducing the amount of drug that is absorbed into the bloodstream; for these medications, you must take the drug at least 1 hour before eating. Other drugs must be taken with or after a meal to reduce the risk of stomach irritation.

WHEN I AM TAKING THE DRUG, DO I NEED TO AVOID ANY OTHER MEDICATIONS OR FOODS?

Some drugs and other substances can have adverse interaction if taken simultaneously. For example, fruit juices reduce the effectiveness of some antibiotics by breaking them down in the stomach. You should avoid drinking alcohol while taking most drugs.

DO I NEED TO TAKE THE FULL COURSE OF TREATMENT?

If you are taking an antibiotic, the infection may return and the bacteria may become resistant if you stop taking the drug before you are supposed to. However, for other drugs it may be acceptable to discontinue treatment as soon as you feel better. Always ask your doctor before you stop taking any drug in advance of the end of the scheduled treatment course.

ARE THERE LIKELY TO BE ANY SIDE EFFECTS AND WHAT SHOULD I DO IF THERE ARE?

Any drug, even aspirin, can cause an adverse reaction in some people. Ask your doctor about expected side effects and possible adverse reactions that can be caused by your medication. If your medication makes you feel dizzy or drowsy, do not drive, operate machinery, or climb ladders. You should report any unexpected side effects to your doctor.

CAN I USE THE DRUG SAFELY OVER A PROLONGED PERIOD OF TIME?

With some drugs there is a possibility of complications with long-term use. For example, some antibiotics, especially when taken for prolonged periods, may result in overgrowth of yeast in the mouth, vagina, or bowel or in infection of the gastrointestinal tract."

PAIN MANAGEMENT

Many people, including patients and health care workers, have a fear of narcotic addiction when it comes to pain medication. However, an irrational fear can cause under-treatment of pain. The health care worker, whether a physician or nurse, must understand the difference between a patient becoming addicted and what an appropriate strategy of pain management should include. This strategy should include helping both the patient and their advocate understand what is appropriate and why.

If you are not the one experiencing the pain it is hard to know the severity and quality of it. Various numbers, as well as physical disposition and verbal queues, can show the body's response to pain. To try and gauge the pain someone is going through you need to find out where the pain is coming from, the intensity and the type.

To find out the intensity, use a scale of zero to ten, with zero being no pain and ten being the worst pain imaginable. In the assessment of pain, the nurses will ask the patient to gauge it on the pain scale, as well as look at the vital signs.

Keep good notes as to when the patient started feeling the pain, how intense it was, what they were doing, when they took medication for the pain, and how it helped relieve the pain. This can not only help the nurses and doctors treat the patient more appropriately, but can help an advocate in providing comfort and understanding. For example, if an advocate knows that the patient previously had a positive reaction to pain medication and how long it took to provide the patient relief, they can use this knowledge in a positive proactive manner to help the patient while the medication takes effect.

It should also be noted that some hospitals actually have pain management teams that are available upon request to help find effective solutions for managing pain."

You should be able to answer all of the following questions with regards to pain. A worksheet is provided in "Appendix E – Pain Management" to help you document this information:

Time of onset?
What is hurting? (Back, stomach, leg, shoulder)
How intense? Scale from (0-10)

> What type of pain? (Cramps, sharp, throbbing, dull, aching, burning, shooting)
> What where they doing? (Walking, sitting, lying)
> Time of pain medication given?
> How did it help?
> How long did the medication work until the pain started again?

Keep in mind that there is a time lag between the time pain medication is given and when it should actually start helping. For example, a drug given by I.V. will help very quickly, often within minutes, versus a medication given by mouth, which could take up to half an hour to start providing relief.

As an advocate, if you have a hard time verbally questioning to find out levels and quality of pain because of a lack of coherency, look for these physical signs:

> **Movement:** Very agitated moving more than normal. Shaking, bending legs, rocking back and forth, restlessness, thrashing, and irritability
> **Sleeplessness:** Can't sleep or very light sleeping
> **Verbal:** Calm, moaning, hysterical
> **Countenance:** The way they look at you, even if they can't verbally say anything. You can see pain is on their face or in their eyes.
> **Appetite:** Loss of.

Stimulation of the five senses (smell, sight, sound, touch, and taste) will, and can, create a diversion that will take the stimulation from the pain receptors and cause the other sensory receptors to become more active. This can help relieve some discomfort. There are natural techniques that stimulate other senses that could greatly help in some medical situations. Some of these techniques are:

Ice (applied or eaten)
Heat
Breathing techniques
Relaxation
Music
Movies/Videos
Family pictures, children drawings
Massages
Lotion that smell good
Good food
Meditation

HOSPITAL CARE FOR PERSONAL HYGIENE

Healthy hygiene includes: bathing (or a bed bath), brushing teeth, washing hair, skin care, and using the bathroom (or bedpan). These things should be provided in a timely manner by the hospital staff. Quality care was not an issue in my mother's former hospital stays. Because there is less nursing staff, no LPN's, and more patients for those nurses, there can be a lack of maintaining quality hygiene.

With my mother's hip surgery four years ago this was never one of my concerns. She had a RN, LPN, and a CNA. This last hospital stay required my diligence to ensure that her hygiene needs were consistently addressed as quickly as possible. The Critical Care Unit had fewer patients, so hygiene needs were addressed fairly consistently depending on who the staff was that day. The last unit, which was for patients going home, to another facility, or to die, was short staffed in all areas. I was constantly walking the halls trying to find a staff member when my mother's call button had been on for five to ten minutes and she was desperate for a bedpan.

I chose to wash and curl my mother's hair since clean and curly hair had always made her feel better and I knew this about her. There is water-free shampoo available that works surprising well. Most hospitals now offer bath cloths, no rinsing needed, which are great for bed baths.

With the decline in hospital staff and the patient-to-nurse ratio increasing, the hygiene care in general is not what it used to be. Speak up when you see neglect in the hygienic care given the patient. Take your concerns to the doctors, as they are the ones that can get the staff moving so that the improvements occur in the patient's care. If it doesn't improve, go to the nursing supervisor, not your nurse.

I know my presence, asking questions, being friendly, and expressing my appreciation for everything that was done for my mother, certainly helped her receive better care than those that did not have someone overseeing what was being done and more importantly, what was not being done.

An older woman, who was across the hall, had an occasional visitor but for the most part spent her time alone. One day during mealtime, I happened to notice she was sitting on the side of the bed throwing up her lunch. I knew she could not walk alone and always had help just getting to a chair. I went to find the nursing assistant, who thanked me, and this good woman had attention for the immediate problem and was prevented from falling over the bed's edge. An advocate needs to also be aware that other patients in the hospital might need your eyes and ears so that they get the care or help they need.

SKIN CARE

Skin is the largest organ of the body. Its health and integrity is essential to life. When one is immobile in a wheelchair or confined to a hospital bed it doesn't take long for one to get a bedsore. Most sores occur within the first few weeks of being confined or immobile. A simple bedsore can become an infected wound that can cause life-threatening infections to spread throughout your entire body. A vast majority of skin breakdown is unnecessary and can be prevented. Skin care is often neglected and should be checked daily to help prevent any breakdown.

Some internal and external factors that can cause skin breakdown are:

External
Temperature (hot, cold)
Chemical (radiation, creams, lotions)
Pressures (constant pressure, restraints)
Moisture (Keep skin dry)
Internal
Medication
Poor nutrition (malnutrition, obesity)
Poor circulation
Swelling of tissues
Changes to supporting structures (decrease in muscle tone, bone loss)
Elasticity of skin compromised (turgor)
Decreased mental awareness

Skin should be clean and odor free. All skin areas should be checked at least once every 24 hours. If one is wearing any type of restraints, the areas under the restraints should be checked for skin breakdown every 4 hours. Breakdown of the skin starts with a red spot, sore to the touch, possibly inflamed, but the skin not broken. This could then progress to the worst case scenario, which is damage to muscle or bone, which is very painful. If caring for, or working with bedsores, be sure to wash your hands to prevent any spreading of infection. Once the skin has been broken, infection is more than likely to be an issue. The sore can become infected very easily. If bedsores are not taken care of quickly they can take a long time (months) to heal. Get care right away on any red spots or open skin. Antibiotics and proper care of the wound will help the skin heal and prevent infection from spreading.

There are many preventive measures available and they should be part of the daily care of the patient. Ask for, and make sure your loved one is receiving, the care needed. Some preventive measures include:

Eating a good diet consisting of high protein and calories.

Rotate positions. While sitting in a chair, move at least every 2 hours. While in a bed, move at least every 4 hours. Use pillows to prop up the patient side to side, or under their legs and arms. Use pillows under legs to keep heels off the bed. Make sure while propping with pillows you don't place them under the patient's knees or armpits as this can cut off circulation.

Rub medicated creams or powder (helps the skin to stay dry) over skin. Don't apply to broken skin.

Egg carton cots (The larger the pocket the better).

Air mattresses. There are many different kinds. Some rotate while different air pockets inflate and deflate, creating variable pressure points.

Wool blankets

As an advocate, encourage skin to be checked and ensure proper care is given.

PHYSICAL THERAPY

Often a patient will require physical therapy, which strengthens and helps the patient regain movement in the limbs, especially after prolonged bed rest, injury, head trauma, stroke, surgery, or illness. Even a bed restricted patient needs physical therapy, which protects against blood clots, and also gives the patient needed movement so that muscle loss is minimized. The doctor gives the order for the patient to receive physical therapy. An individual from physical therapy (PT) will see you, do an evaluation, and then begin therapy.

Within a physical therapy unit or hospital facility there are a variety of machines and equipment designed for the individual inadequacies that a patient might require. Physical therapists use many different devices such as walkers, weights, crutches, grab bars and various belts that secure the therapist and patient when walking.

Some hospitals have access to whirlpools and electro-stimulant therapies.

My mother had physical therapy while hospitalized after her hip surgery. She continued at home during the recovery and then attended an independent physical therapy facility for additional services. For any physical therapy outside of the hospital, you will want to check with the insurance company. Some will pay for this service, and it can be extended when a doctor deems it necessary. Physical therapy can be an important recovery process aid.

As an advocate, if the patent hasn't been able to sit in a chair or get out of bed for 3-5 days, and no physical therapy services have been started, request them! They can, and should, be wearing percussion socks or support hose to ensure proper circulation and prevent blood clots. They should also be participating in some sort of range of motion therapies. These therapies keep good circulation through the legs and other body parts. As with most therapy services, if the patient needs these services during their hospital stay, the therapy is paid for as part of the total bill. Most insurance providers, including Medicare, pay the hospitals a specific amount based on your medical problem.

Ask what you can do for the patient. I can't stress the importance of what the simple act of motion and activity does for the patient's mind and body.

RESPIRATORY AND OCCUPATIONAL THERAPIST

Respiratory Therapists (RT, CRTT, RCP) and Occupational Therapists (OTR) are also part of the health care team. They are not applicable to all situations, but know that they are there and what their role is so that if there is a need, you can make sure you ask for them.

By a physician's order you may see a Respiratory Therapist for breathing tests, breathing treatments, receiving certain medications, and/or other procedures to increase pulmonary function.

Occupational Therapists help with people relearning skills of everyday life. This includes the simple to more advanced tasks, such as eating, getting out of bed, dressing, bathing, and cooking meals. Occupational Therapists help you relearn and/or provide short cuts and energy efficient ways to reclaim these skills in your everyday life.

My mother had occupational therapy while recovering at home from hip surgery. The therapist taught her how to safely enter and exit the shower and how to put on socks and shoes with the aid of a simple device. She used a walker and had a shower seat inside the shower. The occupational therapy gave her needed confidence as she once again began dealing with everyday life.

CHAPTER V
ADVANCE DIRECTIVES

DECISIONAL CAPACITY

Decisional capacity is one's ability to make choices for oneself. Our decisional capacity can become limited due to medication, grief, depression, age, pain, illness or accident. While one is competent is the time for deciding what is right for you in a precarious medical situation.

PROTECT YOUR RIGHTFUL CHOICE

If you are able to make your own decisions and be your own advocate, talk to your physician as to any treatments or life sustaining measurements you wish to have. It is always best if you have it done legally with all required forms filled out as directed. Your doctor does have the authority to write orders as to your wishes. An example of this is a "Do Not Resuscitate" (DNR) order, which means no breathing machines or heart stimulants will be used to keep you breathing and your heart pumping. Another example is a "Treat Arrhythmia's Medically" (TAM) order. This means you cannot be placed on life support machines, such as a ventilator that breathes for you, but you can be given medications to help your heart function. The best scenario for you while you are of sound mind, and not under medication, is to talk with your doctor and fill out legal forms as explained.

My mother had outlined in her living trust what conditions would determine what life support would be administered and also those conditions in which she did not want life support given. Her primary care physician also had a copy of these wishes and a copy was placed in her medical folder that all her doctors used.

My mother had her second bypass surgery for blocked arteries. However, there were other health issues that were not addressed. Because she came into the emergency room in congestive heart failure and had bypass surgery, it improved her general health; however, the primary care doctor and one heart doctor made the decision for the bypass surgery. It sounds logical and the right decision based on the information provided. However, there was no family consultation with the doctors. The primary care doctor and the heart doctor did not consult with the other doctors who had been caring for her over the years.

Does the patient fully understand the doctor's course of treatment? I recognized that my mother was very afraid and not physically healthy enough when this decision was made to voice any questions or concerns. I arrived the morning of surgery. I knew her heart doctor and primary care physician through past medical situations. I trusted their judgment and did not ask for a consultation with all her doctors to weigh the grave decision involving heart surgery for an eighty-two year old woman with other medical problems (some of which hadn't been discovered).

Complex medical crisis have greater health consequences. Thus, information, knowledge, consultations, discussions, and clarity provide a patient/advocate control and input that certainly gives one considerable peace in an often-intense situation. Informed decision-making prompts quality health care, and it perpetuates a higher medical standard. Remember that a patient/advocate has the right to refuse any treatment, surgery or medication.

The following legal documents may be needed for protecting yourself when you can't adequately do so and a trusted relative/ friend/advocate can. Both the DPOA (Durable Power of Attorney) and a Living Will are considered advance directives:

A Durable Power of Attorney

A DPOA is a durable power of attorney that encompasses business, property, and financial decisions, as well as medical decisions. A durable power of attorney for health care (DPOAHC) gives another person you name, the legal authority to make medical decisions in the event you are not able to do so for yourself. You can name a different person for the DPOA and the DPOAHC. For example, you may have a relative that is a doctor you can name for your DPOAHC, and then name someone else in the DPOA to watch over any estate affairs. This includes decisions around life-support and medical treatment. This person should be someone you trust explicitly. You don't need an attorney to make this happen. Most hospitals and health care facilities have forms available. State law may vary so be sure you have the form for your state. Included in the DPOA can also be a directive to the physician. This directive would specify whether medical treatment that only delays death would be withheld, or that treatment should not be withdrawn under any circumstance that would result in death.

Living will

A living will states under what scenarios a patient wants to live or die. A typical will would direct health care workers to withhold life-sustaining measures such as ventilation, tube feeding, etc., in situations that only delay death. A living will details what you want done or not done medically depending on your condition. The living will protects not only you, but also your family member or advocate if you can't speak for yourself or have diminished decisional capacity. Keep in mind that a living will is not legally binding like a DPOA is. Also keep in mind the health care profession is in the business of saving lives and keeping people alive. Be sure to discuss a living will with your physician to ensure you are both on the same page. If your doctor doesn't accept your wishes in the way he practices and looks over your care, get another doctor who does. You should respect the fact that not all physicians may agree with your wishes.

The important information contained in these documents must be your wishes and desires. You need to brainstorm about what you want in different medical crisis situations. You can acquire such help in knowing what you might want in different medical situations from organizations on the Internet or the library. For example, you are bedridden, unable to feed, dress or wash yourself or you are totally dependent on others for your care.

In evaluation of your desire to live or die, you should include these type of considerations as the basis for your decisions (these are just examples):

Living is much worse than death: I don't want life sustaining treatment.

Living is somewhat worse than death: I probably don't want life sustaining treatment.

Living is neither better nor worse than death: I'm not sure I want life sustaining support.

Living is much better than death: I want life sustaining help.

You can obtain living will forms from your lawyer's office, hospital, your doctor's office, or even the Internet. Many hospitals will provide free assistance in filling out these forms. At least a copy of these forms must be kept in your medical records while you are in the hospital. Some hospitals have staff members that are patient care advocates that are available to notarize advance directives.

COMFORT MEASURES

Near the end of life, we sometimes over treat and prolong the inevitable. It is your decision as to what measures you wish to be taken. Instead of prolonging, there is a balance to be struck of relaxing and taking the pain away during those last hours of someone's life. Comfort measures mean you stop all treatments and procedures and simply provide pain relief and basic needs that keep them comfortable.

When it was obvious that my mother was not ever going to recover and keeping her sedated to avoid the extreme abdominal pain was no longer really living, it was time to let her go and have her suffering end. I requested all drugs be stopped except pain medications, and no more breathing treatments or oxygen. Within thirty-six hours of starting comfort measures my mother passed away during the night. The next morning she was to leave the hospital and return home to receive hospice care. She was eighty-two years old and had a full and active life until the last two months.

It can't be expressed how difficult these decisions can be, but it is only fair to the patient to have these comfort measures. In those last hours of life, it becomes a balance between keeping them comfortable and not prolonging the inevitable. If you have any questions, talk with your physician about making the best decision. This can help bring comfort about the difficult decisions that need to be made. Ultimately, you should respect the wishes of your loved one.

COMPLAIN TO WHOM?

My mother went into hip surgery early in the morning. The night before, her doctor spent time with her and later that evening her anesthesiologist paid a visit. My mother had a great fear of surgery. The anesthesiologist said he would order some relaxation medication for her the next morning so she would be calm and relaxed, which he did, and this certainly helped calm her fears. Their visit the night before surgery was very comforting.

My mother went to surgery and I stayed in the waiting area for about 40 minutes. I needed to get something to eat so I left for about 30 minutes. I came back and was told that she did not have surgery

74

and was in recovery. A nurse from recovery came and talked to me. Apparently her heart rate dropped drastically and surgery was stopped. I knew that this took enormous courage on my mother's part to have this operation and she would be devastated to wake up and know that it hadn't taken place. I told the nurse I needed to be at her side when she woke up and I needed to be the one to tell her what had happened. The nurse said, "No," and stated that the policy of the recovery room does not allow for visitors. I tried having her surgeon paged, but he had left the hospital.

She left and I went to the hospital aid at the desk in the waiting room. I explained the situation and explained why I needed to be with my mother when she woke up. This dear woman told me to wait, and she left to talk with someone. She came back and said someone would be coming to speak with me. Soon another dear lady listened to my valued reasons for being with my mother when she woke up. She said, "I'll do what I can." She returned very soon and asked me to follow her down to the recovery room. We went through doors that required a code to enter. I was there when my mother woke up and I was also there to talk to the heart doctor who had been called in to stabilize her heart rate. My mother stayed in the hospital and received a pacemaker. She did have hip surgery two weeks later.

Don't take "no" for the final answer when there is a valid reason for your request. You know the patient better than anyone else. Keep talking to individuals until you find someone who respects your wishes. That doesn't give you the right to be rude, but you can be politely persistent. This is where a doctor's phone number at your fingertips might be needed.

Doctors, nurses, nursing assistants, and all other medical personnel are there to help you. If, after speaking with the nurse, you are still not receiving the care you need, or something is not being taken care of, you can ask for the nursing supervisor and address the issues with him or her. If you are still not satisfied after addressing your concerns with the nursing supervisor, address them to your doctor. Keep in mind, in many cases, these caregivers are simply following hospital policy and procedure and you will likely just have to find the right person in some cases to address your concern. Don't take it personally if someone can't address your concern when it comes to hospital policy.

Anytime there is a great concern about an issue, address it with your doctor. If after a few attempts, and sufficient time, your wishes haven't been met, and you feel it is a very significant issue, seek out the hospital's Medical Director. You can also ask for another doctor to be brought in for a consultation if the present doctor insists on a procedure or care for the patient that doesn't seem to be appropriate.

ETHICAL ISSUES

Physicians not only have a legal obligation to patients, but an ethical one as well. An ethics committee exists if a doctor and/or medical personnel have been asked to do something for a patient that violates the beliefs of the medical staff in doing what is best for the patient. The opposite holds true as well, when the patient feels their beliefs are being compromised. You have the right to ask the Medical Director to call for a convening of an ethics committee. Other medical staff will sit on the board with the Medical Director to listen to both sides of the situation in order to resolve any ethical or moral issues.

CHAPTER VI
SUPPORT

VALUES AND BELIEFS

There is usually a chaplain or clergy in hospitals that you can contact in your time of need. He or she can either contact your religious affiliation or give you spiritual guidance, prayer, and comfort. Ask your nurse to contact him or her. They are at the hospital to be there for you, so don't hesitate. They usually have a great deal of experience in dealing specifically with people enduring medical crisis, so they can be very comforting.

DISCHARGE PLANNERS AND HOSPITAL SOCIAL WORKERS

The hospital Social Services Department is a great resource and ally. The department might have a different name than Social Services (also called Case Management), but they do the same work. They are there for you as well as the patient. If you need someone to talk with, or discuss options regarding a situation you, or the patient are facing, then seek out these people. If they can't help you, they will direct you to who can, or seek out the resources that meet your needs.

Social workers are available for crisis intervention, discharge-planning needs, and can provide information on community support. They can also assist with decisions about appropriate post-hospital care facilities based on your needs.

My mother needed a physical therapist, occupational therapist and a registered nurse to come to her home when she was released from the hospital after her hip surgery. The people from social services put everything in motion. They lined up the professional care and ordered a walker and commode paid for by Medicare. She gave me the address of a place that let us borrow health aid equipment for as long as needed. Resources are available and you can make the situation easier for yourself and the patient if you seek out needed support and help.

HOSPICE COUNCILORS

Hospice provides care and council for dying patients and their families. Upon discharge to hospice care you will be completely informed as to what you need and provided with things in your home or the care facility to meet those needs. A hospice councilor will provide all the needed information. See Chapter 8 for more information about hospice.

INTERPRETERS

If you are struggling to understand because of language barriers, ask for an interpreter. The hospital staff can contact someone to help. With today's technologies, hospitals now have many more resources to overcome various communication barriers. There shouldn't be any charge for these services.

TAKING CARE OF YOU

As an advocate you can (and likely will) become exhausted! You have many concerns and long stays at the hospital take their toll. Just as the patient needs to eat and sleep, so do you. You need breaks. Don't forget your own medications. Too many times the caregiver gives, and gives, and gives until they reach the state of exhaustion. They do this out of love, but you can give the patient much better care and comfort if you take care of yourself. While you are at the hospital, rely on the hospital staff to help where appropriate. Also keep in mind that your energies will be greatly needed when the patient goes home.

Make sure you keep yourself in good physical condition as well. I tried to eat a healthy diet when possible during my mother's hospital stay. I had to work at it, since I didn't have an appetite. I was an avid consumer of water during this time and I used to walk the stairs and the grounds each day to keep physically active. I also ate non-healthy food when I needed such comfort without guilt.

The ordeal of a medical crisis can be both mentally and physically draining. Don't underestimate the impact. Having the support of family and friends who understand the commitment you are making can be a great source of strength.

RESPITE CARE

Respite care provides relief for the caregiver. They will relieve the caregiver from one hour to several days at a time. These services are available in the home and many health care facilities.

PLACES TO STAY

If you are from out of town, or have special circumstances, some hospitals offer family lodging at a low (or no) cost. Some hospitals may allow you to stay in a vacant room for the night. They may also allow you to park your motor home or RV on hospital property. Ask the nurse about any options that might be available for you. While these options may not be available at all hospitals and facilities, it doesn't hurt to ask and understand what options are available when applicable.

CHAPTER VII
INSURANCE

Physicians have become frustrated with the inability to care properly for their patients. Insurance companies have placed restrictions as to the choices of treatments they have. Not all procedures are completely covered under certain insurances. This micromanagement has greatly hindered the flexibility in decision making for the doctors and their patients.

Before the medical emergency arrives, check into supplement medical coverage. My mother had excellent supplement medical insurance that eliminated the financial stress of the situation and gave us one less concern.

Not all care and needs will be covered by Medicare, or insurance companies. Check with them as to all the costs that will be covered, as well as the duration of coverage. Also be sure to double-check with any other insurance companies as well as state providers.

BEWARE: LONG TERM CARE IS NOT CHEAP

Talk to your loved one, find out what they expect and need for the lifestyle they desire. Is it realistic and financially feasible? What

NANCY McCLELLAN & TASI McCLELLAN

are their realistic long-term expectations? Long term health care is expensive and realistic expectations should be set.

VARIOUS INSURANCE PLANS

Medicare
Medicare is a federal insurance program that aids people with their medical expenses from both hospital and other medical bills for those that are 65 years and older or those already receiving Social Security benefits. This federal financial relief is given regardless of income.

To obtain a free copy of "Your Medicare Handbook" Publication #HCFA---10050 visit www.medicare.gov or write to:

US Department of Health and Human Services
Health Care Financing Administration
7500 Security Boulevard
Baltimore, Maryland
21244-1850

Medicaid
Medicaid is both a federal and state insurance program that provides assistance to help pay medical bills for low-income families with limited assets, regardless of age. If you would like more information, contact your county's department of social services about qualifying for this assistance. They will provide you with the details of the program and any necessary paperwork or other requirements.

HMO's
Medicare Health Maintenance Organizations (HMOs) provide health care to enrolled individuals and families in a particular area by physicians who belong to the HMO membership. These physicians

have limited referral authority to outside specialists. There are usually fixed periodic payments to cover the costs of coverage, as well as nominal co-payments at time of treatment. Information on specific coverage and options should obtained through the organization through which the patient is enrolled.

PPO's

Medicare preferred provider organizations (PPOs) are similar to HMOs, but give more flexibility to the patient in seeking out treatment. A patient's doctor need not be in the organization membership to be covered, but there are usually financial advantages to using certain physicians and facilities that this PPO has contracted with an exchanged for reduces fees. This type of insurance will be more expensive than HMO insurance as you pay for the flexibility. As with HMOs, information on specific coverage and options should obtained through the organization through which the patient is enrolled.

Other Types of Insurance

There are many types of insurance, which vary as to what they cover and what you have to pay out of pocket for services. Each has set conditions under which you are covered. Look for the best insurance you can afford while ensuring it meets all your needs. Understand what type of services will likely be allowed under the plan. Here is a list of other type of insurances:

Provider-sponsored organization (PSOs)
Independent practice associations (IPAs)
Group coverage
Individual private coverage
Qualified Medicare Beneficiary
Medical Savings Account (MSA's)

CHAPTER VIII
DISCHARGE FROM THE HOSPITAL

HOME

There really is no place like home. After being discharged the patient will usually have to make a follow up appointment with their PCP/MD at the doctor's office. If they have been given prescriptions for home oxygen or other care, the discharge planner will coordinate with a home health care company to take care of supplies and care needed at home. Keep in mind that most hospitals also have a pharmacy on the premises to allow you to take care of any prescriptions for medicine prior to going home. This can save the time and hassle of traveling to a pharmacy at a later time when you will have more pressing concerns. Home health care companies provide medical and nursing services. They will contact you directly and make appropriate arrangements. Some questions to ask before the patient is discharged home:

New prescriptions- when do they start taking them?
When should they have a follow up appointment?
Who should they see for their follow up appointment?

(Specialist, or my general practitioner.)
If there are any pending tests, where can they obtain the
results?
Is their rehabilitation continued at home?

Also, make sure the patient gets all their personal items back if
they were taken to a secured area when they were admitted. After
several hectic days in a hospital they may not even remember the
fact that their personal belongings are still being stored elsewhere.

HOSPICE

Hospice provides care and comfort in the home, a nursing home,
or assisted living facility. This special care is for those patients and
their families that face a terminal illness where they can no longer
respond to medication or treatment. The concept is to provide and
improve the last days of a patient's life (usually defined as less than
six months to live). It is not intended to prolong nor speed up the
dying process. Hospice deals with pain management, social and
emotional comforts. To enter hospice services you must have a
doctor's referral. The hospice worker you deal with will normally
have been through this experience many, many times and are a great
source of information and comfort that you are doing the right thing
for your loved one. Take advantage of the knowledge and experience
that they possess.

OTHER TYPES OF FACILITIES

Skilled Nursing Facility
These facilities are licensed by the state and require the facilities
to provide physician and rehabilitation services, and also are eligible
for Medicaid reimbursements. These facilities have a staff with 24-
hour nursing care, provide a room, board, and nurses administrating

your medications and other care. Most residents are those with chronic or long-term sicknesses. They are also for individuals just out of the hospital and in need of some additional rehabilitation until they return home. Usually nursing assistants (CNA's) do most of the care, which is supervised by a licensed nurse.

Rehabilitation Units

These units work with stroke patients, spinal cord injuries, brain injuries, and other physical impairment situations. They utilize professionals to help patients relearn and regain a more fulfilling and normal lifestyle.

In hospitals, most rehabilitation units are very aggressive. They provide an environment as if at home. While units may differ slightly, in general they have a physical therapist work with the patient. They will also utilize occupational therapists to help patients learn vital skills while still receiving medical treatment as needed.

Rehabilitation units outside of the hospital are usually not as aggressive. These units are usually a skilled nursing facility, which provide a physical therapist to work with the patient. These facilities do provide medical treatments, but not at the level that would be available in a hospital rehabilitation unit. Usually there are no services from a licensed specialist such as a respiratory therapist.

Transitional Care Unit (TCU)

Usually found in hospitals, it is just a step from hospital to home with minimal nursing staff, to provide medication, dressing changes and toiletry needs. Physical therapists are available on an as needed basis.

Assisted Living Residence/Residential Care

Depending on the state, these facilities may or may not be licensed. The vast majority (approximately 90%) are paid by individual funds. The Medicaid program is now reimbursing some facilities. These facilities differ in what they offer, so check with the individual facilities for information. General lists of services at these facilities are:

> 24 hour staff
> Shared, or private rooms
> Meals served in a dining room
> Social activated
> Recreational activities
> Provide transportation local shopping centers
> Housekeeping services
> Laundry services
> Medication reminders

In Home Care With Professional Assistance

In these cases either a registered nurse or a licensed practical nurse, will come in and check vitals (temperature, blood pressure, oxygenation, heart rate, respiratory rate, etc.) and do those things that your physician feels are necessary. They administer medications and take care of any personal hygiene that is needed.

Usually they don't do any laundry or cooking, etc. It is strictly medical and hygienic care. In these situations an occupational therapist or physical therapist may visit to provide aid and teach skills to make home life a good experience. Insurance coverage will usually determine the type of care one can receive in the at home environment.

CHAPTER IX
FUNERAL ARRANGEMENTS

Upon the death of an individual, the hospital or care center will need to know the mortuary that will claim the body. Certainly, the ideal situation is that open discussions concerning such matters are clearly known by the advocate, friend, or relative of the deceased. Most people are uncomfortable with such matters and the elderly tend to shy away from this kind of dialogue.

One can learn about local mortuaries from the neighbors, friends and relatives of the individual. When talking of a friend or of a patient that has died recently, one can guide the conversation about the deceased's funeral, mortuary and other arrangements. Adding your own personal preference about these matters might encourage the open communication that gleams information that gives you peace about the arrangements you might make.

A mortuary can provide you a price list, which will also list various other services they may provide. Comparison-shopping among the various mortuaries can save money. The greatest expense is the casket. Remember that the casket serves the same function whether it is expensive or inexpensive. We had done some comparison-shopping when we decided on the mortuary that would handle my mother's funeral. They even had the same casket we had wanted. There was one problem. They wanted $600 more. Since we had information and could quote the casket price that the other mortuary had offered, our mortuary agreed to that price also. When choosing cremation you must also decide what is to be done with the ashes. A reputable mortuary is helpful and respectful of your wishes. There should be no heavy-handed pressure or dialogue that invokes guilt for the choices you have made. Find another mortuary if you feel uncomfortable in any way in this situation.

Make a list of the basics that you know you want for sure. Then let the funeral director guide you through information as to any changes or additions you might decide upon. The funeral director will require personal information on the deceased. Social security number, date and place of birth, father and mother's name, and the date and place of death are usually necessary. If possible, have someone go with you to the mortuary.

The mortuary can get death certificates right away. There is a fee to get copies of the death certificate. However, it is very important that you order extra at this time otherwise you could wait months while the county processes the information. My mother's personal business accounts each needed a death certificate as part of the estate settlement. All banking institutions will need a death certificate in order to transfer accounts. You will also need copies for stocks, bonds, titles, insurance, social security, military and the presently unknown. My mother had a living will yet we used all but a few of the extra death certificates that we obtained.

An obituary is a good idea when having a funeral or graveside service. It informs the public that a member of the community is deceased. My mother had a dear friend that I didn't know how to get a hold of and fortunately she saw the obituary and was able to attend the funeral.

Lights in the home that come off and on at different times will protect the property when the homeowner is in a serious medical condition and the property is empty. During the funeral it is wise to have a neighbor watch the home or someone stay in the home during this time as you would be surprised how criminals prey on those that are mourning. The mortuary can provide an outline to help in the obituary's format. The number of words determines the cost for the obituary and it can be expensive. Most newspapers will publish a short notice for free.

During this time, the deceased has been the main focus for a duration that could be short or long, but that type of intense focus is now no longer present. Upon their death and after their affairs are in order, the grieving process might be more intense than in normal circumstances had you not been the advocate/relative. Recognize your own vulnerability as related to the unique situation you have experienced. You were involved in life and death decisions for another person. That is an intense circumstance in ones personal life. Now the focus is you. Get help and counseling if needed during this grieving process. There are many support sources available such as friends, family, clergy and professional grief counselors.

As you get the deceased's affairs in order, pay close attention to any activity that seems out of the ordinary. Three months after my mother's death we received a credit card bill. Upon contacting the bank we learned that one does not need the actual card to use for a purchase, but just having the number is enough, especially with phone or Internet orders. As statements arrived we wrote right on the statement that the card needed to be cancelled, as the person was now deceased. Make a list of all credit cards, needed insurance information, titles and other legal documents of your friend or family member. This would also be an excellent practice for anyone so that in a medical emergency, or life-threatening situation those that must deal with your personal affairs have everything in order. Older senior citizens get very protective about their personal financial business, so be respectful and explain why such measures give them protection against someone taking advantage of them when a medical emergency arises.

Income tax can be assessed for three years after someone has died. Keep all tax records from at least the last three years of the deceased person's life. Having to dig up this information three years later will not be a pleasant experience for you.

Keep all receipts and bills pertaining to the expenses of the estate, such as lawyer fees, funeral expenses, repairs on a house to sell, outstanding bills that are paid and anything that is directly related to the affairs of the deceased person. These can be deducted from the estate's total worth for tax purposes. There are often medical expenses not covered by the deceased's medical insurance that are unknown immediately following their death, but will likely surface via bills in the mail in the following months.

This is also a time to take care of you after taking care of another in this demanding and trying circumstance. NO ONE can understand what you have gone through when you are an advocate for a person in a serious medical situation, except another advocate. The service and care you have rendered is remarkable and invaluable. You are an advocate.

DEFINITIONS

Artery: One of the vessels carrying oxygenated blood from the heart to the tissues (one exeption: pulmonary arteries.)

B.i.d: 2 times a day

BS: Bachelor of Science; Bachelor of Surgery

BSN: Bachelor of Science in Nursing

CCM: Certified Case Manager

CCRN: Certified Critical Care Registered Nurse

CEN: Certified Emergency Nurse

CIC: Certified Infection Control Nurse

CNA: Certified Nursing Assistant; Certified in Nursing Administration: Take approximately a six-week course to become certified to provide personal care to patients. Some of duties include bathing, dressing, and toileting, taking vitals. Work under a licensed nurse

CPN: Certified Pediatric Nurse

CRNH: Certified Registered Hospice Nurse

CRTT: Certified Respiratory Therapy Technician: Less schooling than a RRT.

CWCN: Certified Wound Care Nurse

DO: Doctor of Osteopathy; Doctor of Optometry

DP: Doctor of Pharmacy

DrPH: Doctor of Public Health

DS: Doctor of Science

EENT: eyes, ears, nose and throat

EMT: Emergency Medical Technician

FNP: Family Nurse Practitioner

FP: Family Practitioner

LPN: Licensed Practical Nurse: A person who has undergone training, one year of college courses and passed a state-licensing test. Provides routine care for the sick, administer some medications, change dressings.

LVN: Licensed Visiting Nurse; Licensed Vocational Nurse: Same as an LPN

MD: Doctor of Medicine

Mpharm: Master in Pharmacy

MSurg: Master of Surgery

NMT: Nurse Massage Therapist

NP: Nurse Practitioner

Nursing: Health-care profession providing physical and emotional care to the sick and disabled and promoting health in all individuals through activities including research, health education, and patient consultation

OCN: Oncology Certified Nurse

OTR: Registered Occupational Therapist

PA: Physician's Assistant

PD: Doctor of Pharmacy

PT: Physical Therapist

Physical Therapy: The treatment of disease by physical and mechanical means (as massage, regulated exercise, water, light, heat, and electricity)

Q.i.d: Four times a day

Q2h: Every two hours

Q3h: Every three hours

RD: Registered Dietician

RN: Registered Nurse: Minimum two years of college courses, a graduate trained nurse who has been tested and licensed by a state.

To provide highly skilled medical care to patients. Administer medications and work with doctors to provide care to patients.

RPh: Registered Pharmacist

RPT: Registered Physical Therapist

RRT: Registered Respiratory Therapist RRT/RCP: specialized schooling in pulmonary function. Provided treatments and tests to improve the pulmonary functions.

Stat: Immediately

T.i.d: Three times a day

Transportation Technician: Within the hospital, transportation technicians assist in the transporting of individuals from room to room, or to tests throughout the hospital. It is not required for these individuals to have any medical background.

Veins: A vessel carring deoxygenated blood from tissues back to the heart (one exeption pulmonary veins.)

RESOURCES

Use medical libraries at hospitals and universities. Remember to check dates of references materials, medicine changes very quickly in today's world.

Internet Resources:

http://www.infotrieve.com/search/docsource.asp
http://www.os.dhhs.gov/
http://www.ncbi.nlm.nih.gov/entrez/query.fcgi?tool=infotrieve
http://www.nlm.nih.gov/medlineplus/
http://www.pharmacy.org/
www.my.webmd.com
www.quackwatch.com
www.fda.gov
www.PDR.net
www.emedguides.com
www.gateway.nlm.nih.gov
www.aha.org
www.familydoctor.org

Book resources

A source for elder care at home. *THE COMPLETE ELDERCARE PLANNER*, Joy Loverde.

GONE FROM MY SIGHT- THE DYING EXPERIENCE, Barbara Karnes(RN), Stillwell Kansas. Copyright 1986.

Other Resources:

American Board of Medical Specialists
(800) 776-2378

Department of Corporations (for HMO patients)
(800) 400-0815

Department of Health Services
(916) 445-2070

Health and Human Services Fraud
(800) 447-8477

Medicare General Information Line
(800) 772-1213

Social Service Issues
(800) 269-0271

Appendix A:

Please visit www.publishamerica.com, under our book title to download printable worksheets.

DAILY LOG			
DAY: _____		DATE: _____	

	MORNING	AFTERNOON	EVENING
NURSE'S NAME:			
ASSISTANT'S NAME:			

QUESTIONS TO ASK MD:

1) _____

2) _____

3) _____

4) _____

5) _____

TO DO LIST FOR ADVOCATE (EX., CANCEL APPOINTMENTS, FEED ANIMALS, WATER PLANTS)

1) _____

2) _____

3) _____

4) _____

5) _____

Appendix B

HOSPITAL ADMITTANCE CHECKLIST
☐ NOTEBOOK
☐ PENCIL
☐ LIST OF AT HOME MEDICATIONS (INCLUDING OVER THE COUNTER)
☐ LIST OF ALLERGIES
☐ DOCTOR'S NAME/PRACTICE/PHONE NUMBERS
☐ SOCIAL SECURITY NUMBER
☐ MEDICAL INSURANCE INFORMATION
☐ FAMILY/FRIENDS TELEPHONE NUMBERS
☐ ADVANCE DIRECTIVES

Appendix C

PATIENT INFORMATION

HOME ADDRESS: _____ HOME PHONE: _____

SS NUMBER: _____ DOB: _____ WORK PHONE: _____

ADVOCATE NAME: _____ ADV HOME PHONE: _____

ADV CELL PHONE: _____ ADV PAGER: _____ ADV WORK PHONE: _____

HOSPITAL NAME: _____

HOSPITAL ROOM #: _____ HOSPITAL PHONE NUMBER: _____

INSURANCE COMPANY: _____ POLICY #: _____

CONTACT NAME: _____ INSURANCE PHONE NUMBER: _____

DOCTOR'S NAME: _____ PRACTICE NAME: _____

OFFICE PHONE #: _____ DOCTOR'S PAGER #: _____

DOCTOR'S NAME: _____ PRACTICE NAME: _____

OFFICE PHONE #: _____ DOCTOR'S PAGER #: _____

DOCTOR'S NAME: _____ PRACTICE NAME: _____

OFFICE PHONE #: _____ DOCTOR'S PAGER #: _____

CURRENT USE OF PRESCRIBED AND OVER THE COUNTER MEDICATIONS

NAME: _____ FREQ.: _____ DOSE: _____

NAME: _____ FREQ.: _____ DOSE: _____

NAME: _____ FREQ.: _____ DOSE: _____

NAME: _____ FREQ.: _____ DOSE: _____

OTHER ALTERNATIVE REMEDIES OR SUPPLEMENTS

VITAMINS/HERBS: _____

ALLERGIES: _____

HISTORY OF PAST SURGERIES

SURGERY: _____ DATE: _____

SURGERY: _____ DATE: _____

SURGERY: _____ DATE: _____

ADVANCE DIRECTIVE ON FILE (YES/NO): _____ TYPE: _____

99

PATIENT NETWORK INFORMATION

NAME: _____ RELATIONSHIP: _____

HOME ADDRESS: _____

HOME PHONE: _____ CELL PHONE: _____ PAGER: _____

NAME: _____ RELATIONSHIP: _____

HOME ADDRESS: _____

HOME PHONE: _____ CELL PHONE: _____ PAGER: _____

NAME: _____ RELATIONSHIP: _____

HOME ADDRESS: _____

HOME PHONE: _____ CELL PHONE: _____ PAGER: _____

NAME: _____ RELATIONSHIP: _____

HOME ADDRESS: _____

HOME PHONE: _____ CELL PHONE: _____ PAGER: _____

NAME: _____ RELATIONSHIP: _____

HOME ADDRESS: _____

HOME PHONE: _____ CELL PHONE: _____ PAGER: _____

NAME: _____ RELATIONSHIP: _____

HOME ADDRESS: _____

HOME PHONE: _____ CELL PHONE: _____ PAGER: _____

NAME: _____ RELATIONSHIP: _____

HOME ADDRESS: _____

HOME PHONE: _____ CELL PHONE: _____ PAGER: _____

NAME: _____ RELATIONSHIP: _____

HOME ADDRESS: _____

HOME PHONE: _____ CELL PHONE: _____ PAGER: _____

NAME: _____ RELATIONSHIP: _____

HOME ADDRESS: _____

HOME PHONE: _____ CELL PHONE: _____ PAGER: _____

Appendix D

DRUGS AND THE CENTRAL NERVOUS SYSTEM

DRUG NAME	NORMAL		WHAT I'M TAKING	
	FREQUENCY	DOSE	FREQUENCY	DOSE
1)				
2)				
3)				
4)				

DRUGS FOR DIGESTIVE DISORDERS

DRUG NAME	NORMAL		WHAT I'M TAKING	
	FREQUENCY	DOSE	FREQUENCY	DOSE
1)				
2)				
3)				
4)				

DRUGS FOR HEART AND CIRCULATION

DRUG NAME	NORMAL		WHAT I'M TAKING	
	FREQUENCY	DOSE	FREQUENCY	DOSE
1)				
2)				
3)				
4)				

DRUGS FOR RESPIRATORY DISORDERS

DRUG NAME	NORMAL		WHAT I'M TAKING	
	FREQUENCY	DOSE	FREQUENCY	DOSE
1)				
2)				
3)				
4)				

DRUGS FOR PAIN AND INFLAMMATION

DRUG NAME	NORMAL		WHAT I'M TAKING	
	FREQUENCY	DOSE	FREQUENCY	DOSE
1)				
2)				
3)				
4)				

DRUGS FOR INFECTION AND INFESTATIONS

DRUG NAME	NORMAL		WHAT I'M TAKING	
	FREQUENCY	DOSE	FREQUENCY	DOSE
1)				
2)				
3)				
4)				

DRUGS FOR HORMONAL DISORDERS

DRUG NAME	NORMAL		WHAT I'M TAKING	
	FREQUENCY	DOSE	FREQUENCY	DOSE
1)				
2)				
3)				
4)				

ANTI-CANCER DRUGS

DRUG NAME	NORMAL		WHAT I'M TAKING	
	FREQUENCY	DOSE	FREQUENCY	DOSE
1)				
2)				
3)				
4)				

DRUGS FOR EYES, EARS, AND SKIN DISORDERS

DRUG NAME	NORMAL		WHAT I'M TAKING	
	FREQUENCY	DOSE	FREQUENCY	DOSE
1)				
2)				
3)				
4)				

Appendix E

PAIN MANAGEMENT	
TIME OF ONSET?	
HOW INTENSE (1-10)?	
WHAT IS HURTING? (LEG, BACK, STOMACH, CHEST, ETC.)	
WHAT TYPE OF PAIN? (CRAMP, THROBBING, ACHING, BURNING, SHOOTING, ETC.)	
WHAT WERE YOU DOING? (WALKING, SITTING, LYING, EATING, ETC.)	
TIME PAIN MEDICATION WAS GIVEN?	
HOW DID IT HELP YOUR PAIN (0-10)?	
HOW LONG DID THE PAIN MEDICATION WORK BEFORE IT STARTED AGAIN?	